David Agness

FISHING ADVENTURES ON THE FLY

with Dave and Lindsay Agness

Table of Contents

Foreword i

1. When a Plan Comes Together 1

2. My Fishing Partner: 11

3. Fat Albert & "MEDIUM" Lodging 22

4. My First Time (in Alaska) 34

5. Salty Silvers (Prince William Sound Alaska) 44

6. End of the World Steelhead 52

7. Playing Nicely With Bears 66

8. Out Numbered By The Fairer Sex In Alaska 78

9. The Haunting 92

10. Keeler Fly 101

11. "Getting into the Swing of things" 110

12. Small Streams and Trickles 122

13. A Day To Remember For Ever 129

14. Was Hot, but Now.....I'm Not 134

15. Karma 138

16. Labrador 146

Foreword

I'M JUST A fisherman. Not a trout or fishing bum. Lindsay and I have spent over 40 years in manufacturing and corporate America but outside of our family, spend most of our adventurous moments trying to catch fresh and salt water fish on a fly.

I've been a USCG Licensed Charter Boat Captain and guided anglers for over 20 years. Lindsay is currently a New York State Licensed Fly Fishing Guide. I eventually gave up guiding on Lake Ontario to spend more time traveling and fishing for fun and adventure.

We dedicate our time I used to spend guiding to now volunteering for the improvement of fisheries, by doing projects with Trout Unlimited. And finally we've been deeply involved with Project Healing Waters, and Oasis Adaptive Sports, two Veterans organizations using fly fishing as therapy for wounded and injured Soldiers. And then Casting for Recovery (CFR) which also uses fly fishing as therapy for recovering breast cancer patients. Honestly these activities have turned out to be the most amazing experiences of our lives. Doing our best to give back to these honorable men and women who put their lives on the line every day for our country and the equally brave women on their journey through recovery from breast cancer

My passion for fishing stems from my dad and grandfather. Like many young folks who are introduced to fishing and hunting, I came along the traditional route of having a father and grandfather whose culture was the outdoors. That, and the fact my best friend Dan and I lived to fish which was a disadvantage to our school work back in middle school and had an impact on our focus for anything else BUT fishing. I'm dedicating this effort to my Dad. He wasn't a fancy angler. Never fished with the best gear, or in the most exotic places, he just could flat out fish. He taught me not only the skills of angling, but way more important, he taught me to appreciate the freedom we have to fish and hunt, and to enjoy the places where fish live. Most of all he taught me to respect the animals we hunt, and the fish we fish for.

This First essay is the one and only not about fly fishing. But rather a story that was somewhat of a minor miracle in the scheme of things when planning a trip a year in advance, in hopes that it works out. I now do believe in miracles.

When a Plan Comes Together

"HOLY SHIT...I JUST got a look at him...I almost wish I hadn't seen the size of him he's big'...my father's words hung in the cold crisp Oct air as he leaned against the mahogany gunnels of the "48" Chris Craft. Rod bent double as a large Musky was lunging under the port chine in hopes of rubbing the lure and line free of his sore mouth. Our Guide Jim barked instructions at the old man, but the old man was truly an "Old Man of the Sea' who had fought countless big fish from the Great Lakes to Alaska, he knew what to do, so as the fish sounded beneath the wooden hull dad dipped the rod to the cork in the water to make sure the fish would swim free of the hull and skeg off the stern of the boat.

An idea popped into my head about five weeks before Christmas in 1990. My dad was at an age and stage in his life where he had everything he could ever want or need. I was running a charter fishing operation out on Lake Ontario at the time, so if I bought him more fishing gear, the family would tease that I was just shopping eventually for myself, as dad would pass the gear along to me at some point. I wanted to get him something unique, something he'd treasure for a long time.

My father had fished from the Great Lakes to Alaska in his life, caught countless bass, pike, salmon and trout not to mention pan fish, but he'd never caught a Musky. My memory kicked in of a time in the Thousand Islands around a little inlet called Fisher's Landing, while on vacation with my father and grandfather where we spied this huge fish laying in the shallows. My dad and grandfather knew right away it was a large Musky and my dad spent time casting plugs, spoons and spinners at this great fish to no avail.

That's it, I'd try to fill out the old man's dance card and get him a Musky trip with a famous guide on a classic 1000 Islands wooden guide skiff. Since we had spent over twenty years fishing the 1000 islands together, I already knew of the guide I wanted if I could get him. A salty old native of the islands named Jim Braubant.

Jim had a classic 1948 Chris Craft Sea Skiff 28 feet in length with twin Gray marine engines. The boat was impeccable. For as much as my father and I loved fishing, we loved boats and classic boats much more. Jim had a reputation as a great Musky Guide. I got Jim's number and gave him a call.

The phone conversation was just as I imagined, a gravelly voice told me stories of good times to come and big fish he'd caught over the past 30 years of guiding in that time frame. I asked him to send me a brochure and a note to my dad saying Merry Christmas and can't wait to fish with you next Oct 19! October 19, this was Thanksgiving 1990 the trip was almost a year away but hell that's when Musky fishing was happening in the Islands. Seemed odd to give a gift the receiver won't cash in for almost 11 months after they receive it.

But I knew it would be well received. A few days later the brochure came in the mail. By then I had decided to get a Musky fishing book for dad to read to kind of get him excited about the trip. I selected a fantastic book titled "Before I forget" 50 years of Musky fishing by Len Hartman who did the majority of his fishing in the 1000 islands right where we were headed. I packaged everything up, the book, the brochure, wrote a little note to my father and got ready for Christmas Eve.

All families have rituals on Christmas Eve. For us it was going to mass at 5 PM, return home about 6 PM *since we'd sneak out during communion*, have some drinks, and snacks, a nice dinner, and then open gifts. You can imagine the grand kids waiting for all that stuff to happen before they could get their hands on presents. We still had a few believers in the bunch so we had to be careful on how the presents arrived, however we all knew they came by way of a little red sleigh eight tiny reindeer and a fat jolly little man. But this night I was more antsy then the kids. I wanted to get to the present part of the night. Finally it was time to open gifts. The kids tear into packages like coming out of a shot gun start at a bass tournament, but as things settled down to a roar, I handed dad this package.

He opened it up, at first was shocked to see that I had booked him a charter trip. He was thrilled. But it was still more than 10 months away. No matter, we always used to schedule fishing trips very early in the New Year and then get together for months on end to plan them out. This was no different. I'd stop in for a beer with the old man, he'd be referring to Hartman's book, or we'd go out to some tackle store and he'd look at the Musky baits. As we got into August, he was eager to book a motel for the night before the fishing trip. The trip was on a Friday. I planned it that way in case we had a blow off day, because the guide also had Saturday open. Plan was to head up to Clayton in the 1000 islands on Thursday Oct. 18.

We decided to take Dad's Van. One of those classy one's back in the day with the carpeted floor and walls, swivel chairs, and a couch in the back. We loved to knock around the 1000 Islands. There was always a beer and a sandwich at Roxy's in Cape Vincent, many tackle stores to stop in and shoot the breeze, as well as other fine adult beverage establishments where the talk of the day in Oct. could be everything from Musky fishing, to the duck hunting going on up there. In reality, probably more like people on assistance after the last tourists of the season had left figuring out how to make ends meet until they could get back to their jobs waiting tables, filling boats at the town gas dock, or working in the many shops that lined the streets of the three main towns, Cape Vincent, Clayton, and Alexander Bay.

It was still dark as we left for the Islands. Heading down RT 104 on a Thursday morning we got tangled up in the traffic heading off to work at the nearby Xerox plant. Once out of town we didn't see many cars. It would have been an easy drive, except for one thing.

THE WEATHER. There is just noting that can drag you down farther when the adrenalin of anticipation races through your veins for an exciting journey you are about to embark on, then to have poor weather conditions. Poor at that moment was softening the blow. IT WAS SNOWING.

The further north east we traveled the bigger the flakes. We'd fiddle with the radio the whole ride up trying to find a weather report for the next day for any sign of a weather change. I drove the van while dad relaxed or at least pretended to relax. One eye on the road the other on the sky. We searched at day light for any sign of a break in the weather peering behind us for clear sky to no avail. We arrived in the Cape and like clockwork strutted up to the bar in the Roxy. Ordered a couple drinks, and looked for the opportunity to ask the bartender the question we could only cross our fingers in hoping to hear for an answer. 'So what's the weather supposed to look like tomorrow"?

As you ride into Cape Vincent, the first thing that catches your eye where RT 12E makes a 90 degree turn into town is the St Lawrence River. In all its glory she was dark blue, foamed in white caps, five to six footers as the gusty NE wind whipped her into a froth. Every place we went, we didn't get the answer we hoped for. Either an "I don't know"…or "More of the Same". After each stop we'd walk back out to get in the van and crane our necks looking for any sign possible that this was just a one day event.

We drove down to where the old 48 Chris Craft was gently rocking in her boat house slip protected from the wind, and snow. She was magnificent! Shiny mahogany, so shiny you could shave in its reflection along the study free boards. We didn't step down into her, as we hadn't been officially piped aboard. Side by side sat two engine covers housing the twin Gray Marines. We knew all too well with the mufflers on these old rigs like the Chris Crafts, and Lyman's the engines rumbled to life, and sang a low baritone beat as they idled.

The wind was still whistling and we trekked back to the van to make our next Stop at O'Brian's. A late day whiskey might take our mind off the weather, but not likely. We made the robotic comment about the weather to the bar keep to which she replied, well it's supposed to clear up for tomorrow and be nice". I didn't know whether to scream at her for playing with us, or lean over the bar and kiss her. Of course we didn't let her comments about the weather slip past us. We ran a full court press on her to give us some detail, some proof there was a chance even if remote that the wind would die down. We'd deal with rain, sleet or snow as long as the river would calm down.

"No really" she said. "I just heard they changed the weather report for tomorrow, going to be Sunny and nice." I looked at dad and he looked at me, this is a nice lady and she's said twice it was going to get nice, she couldn't possibly be pulling our leg. But then again she knew we weren't locals. Dad and I were typical out of towner's where everybody is trained in a resort area, to always spin the positive. But hell it was late Oct. we couldn't be your typical tourists.

The evening before the almost year long wait approached. We had spent the day knocking around the three towns riding the edges of the mighty St. Lawrence visiting the few merchants and establishments that remained open this late in the season. Time for dinner and after a delicious meal we stepped outside and to my amazement for the first time all day the wind seemed to have slowed to a stiff breeze from a howling gale. Maybe the nice lady in O'Brien's was going to get this right.

Off to sleep, me with my brain only half turned down, the other half a radar sweeping for the sound of wind 10 feet outside our motel door. Finally sleep got the better of me and the night fell silent. 5:30 AM the little portable alarm rousted us out of the rack and my first movement was for the door. Dad was rubbing his eyes, shaking the cobwebs loose and causally asked, "What's it look like out there'. I turned to him with the chilly air rushing in the door "There isn't a breath of wind out there and the sky is filled with stars". Suddenly the old man's eyes flashed a brilliance and level of attention you'd expect after the first cup of coffee or two. We quickly got dressed and headed off for Breakfast.

As we pulled into the marina about 30 minutes before our expected departure of 8 AM, there was Capt. Jim in no hurry and at a very relaxed pace moving about the old Sea Skiff sipping coffee and pulling out his tackle. Rods, reels, huge swim and trolling plugs, some with distinct bite marks on them signaling these had been bitten by Musky's.

What happened next was one of the highlights for dad and I, one we hadn't probably discussed yet both of us looked forward to, was the moment Capt. Jim put the keys in the ignitions of those two gray marines and fired them to life. The loud report of the engines through the mufflers makes an impression and then the slow rumble of the idle as they wind away waiting to perform their duty. I saw a smile cross the old man's face. I could see his mind wander back to years of owning old wooden boats that sounded just like this treasure of a platform.

Capt. Jim welcomed us aboard and as we backed out of the boat house it was like a spot light was thrust down on us. The bright sunshine sending considerable warmth across our shoulders. Capt. Jim threw the throttles in gear, the tranny's as smooth as butter slipped us forward into the refreshing breeze against our cheeks as we chugged up the channel.

"We are going to run over to 40 acre shoals and troll the drop-offs" said Capt. Jim. The old man had fished this place as a kid with my grandfather, and 40 Acre Shoal was a favorite of Len Harman the famous Musky man we had been reading about the past 10 months. Once in the river proper, Capt. Jim ran the engines up to three quarters and we slid across the flat surface where yesterday five footers and foam from cresting waves marched from the east to the west bank of this mighty river.

A short 20 minute ride to the shoal, sun shining and the temperature raising quickly with the warmth of the enclosed cabin on the Sea Skiff and we were shedding coats hats and gloves. Dad was the kind of guy who could get in a conversation with anybody at any time. He was a master of having a new acquaintance open up his life story for show and tell. Capt. Jim rattled along on his 30 years of guiding with

Dad firing off the next question like putting a fresh log on the fire to keep the conversation going. Jim is the consummate guide telling stories of big Musky's, while mixing in stories of his past growing up on Grindstone island and a lifetime of living in this magnificent place all the while setting lines. Finally all lines in, we started a slow troll along a steep drop off where Jim had caught countless monsters.

When I decided to embark on this adventure, I knew we were going after the fish of 10,000 casts or 1000 hours of chase to get one good shot. It was one huge win to actually be out on the water after the weather the day before but it was almost too much to ask for success in getting a hit let alone actually land a musky. We had a one day charter in the third week of October setup a year before in hopes of getting that ONE shot.

My dad loved to fish and catch fish, but in our life time fishing together, he was never a numbers guy, never meant much to him. He truly knew how to enjoy every detail of a fishing trip and while we of course wanted to actually catch a Musky, the fact that we were fishing for them was the summit of the Musky mountain we had hoped to climb.

10:25 AM, Capt. Jim knew that I was also a USCG licensed Charter Capt. He also knew I had years of experience of my own handling the type of gear including the downriggers we were fishing. He asked me to lower one of his sets a few feet while he kept the boat on course. I walked to the back of the boat, dropped the bait to his commanded depth, loaded the rod in the rod holder against the release clip and eased back into my seat.

10:30, that same rod I had just re-adjusted rocketed off and instinctively (as I do on my own Charter Boat) I was ON IT in a split second pure reflex from years of setting hooks on fish from a released downrigger. I struck the fish hard and immediately felt the weight of the fish and the rod bowed to the water.

I turned and yelled to my father to take the rod, but dad was already right behind me so the hand off was quick and smooth. At the same moment Jim ripped the throttles back into neutral as tried and true Musky guides will not pull a Musky that is hooked. It's all up to the angler and the fish, moreover he shut the engines down and the day fell silent as the flat calm river simply hugged the hull of the old 48.

The fish didn't jump, rather pulled line off the drag heading in the opposite direction. My father was a highly experienced angler with regards to pumping and reeling in a big fish and Dad effortlessly spun this big toothy critter towards the boat but Musky's even with a small brain aren't stupid and this fish charged the boat still no sight of him until.....

" Holy Shit, I just got a look at him. I almost wish I hadn't seen the size of him he's big", my father's words hung in the cold crisp October air and he leaned against the mahogany gunnels of the 48 Chris Craft. Rod bent double as a large Musky was lunging under the port chine in hopes of rubbing the lure and line free of his sore mouth. The Guide barked instructions at the old man, but the old man was truly an "Old man of the Sea' who had fought countless big fish from the great lakes to Alaska. He knew what to do, so as the fish sounded beneath the wooden hull, dad dipped the rod in the water to make sure the fish would clear the hull and skeg off the stern of the boat.

Finally the Musky in the 35-40 pound range was alongside the boat. Engines silent, quietly rocking on the sleepy half foot roll, Guide Jim netted the fish, and gently lifted her onto the deck. Hooks were freed and the fish was measured at 50 inches, pictures snapped and swiftly returned to the river.

Needless to say the yelps and high fives and back slapping went on for several minutes. I turned to Jim and smiled "I thought this Musky fishing thing was supposed to be very difficult, fish of a 10,000 casts or a 1000 hours of trolling we've only been out here two hours, to which I got the expected response that might be the only bite we get all day (and it was by the way)...and that we were fortunate.

Of course my dad being my dad started saying you should have kept the rod I would have liked to see you catch that fish but he wasn't as convincing as he usually was because he knew it was my dream for the past year to come up there and get him his Holy Grail. I was overwhelmed that this project had worked out. That the stars all aligned for this man who I loved with all my heart, who was my dad and my best friend. A lifelong fishing partner who had spent countless hours of his time taking me and my buddies to this magical place, the 1000 islands. For many years let alone the countless trips we had made fishing around home......FINALLLY...I was able to provide the adventure for HIM...

I thanked God. I thanked Capt. Jim, if the bartender gal from O'Brien's who gave us the REAL weather forecast was onboard, I would have hugged and thanked her as well. You put a trip together a year ahead of time to travel and fish in a time frame where weather can shut you down in a minute. Then to fish for the hardest fish to catch in these waters, hope for just a strike and a glimpse of one of these brutes let alone land one, and it all happened as planned... on a day... that resembled a late May Friday afternoon....not the end of Oct.....

The old man and I have a ritual after a great day of fishing. We seek a classic whiskey, and a fine dinner. On the trip back to Rochester, we pulled off at a little road side restaurant that had a reputation for having the elements we sought to end the day. With a couple double shot rock glasses I lifted in his honor and toasted my dad and his Musky.

Couple of sub notes that are interesting. On the St. Lawrence River in the 1000 islands there is a Conservation group. The "Save The River Foundation". One aspect this foundation is noted for if an angler releases a legal Musky (back in 1991 a legal Musky was 46 inches or greater) the angler would receive a beautiful print by James Ringer an artist in that area of a Musky, and they would report the catch in the local newspaper the 1000 Island Sun. Those things were awarded my dad, and we framed the print.

That print, since his passing away now hangs in my house. Maybe even greater is that Capt. Jim donated his 28 foot 1948 Chris Craft to the world famous Antique Boat Museum in Clayton New York. So if you visit the Museum you can see the boat in all its magnificence. For me I get to relive that special day as I climb the steps alongside this vessel where a wide smile breaks across my face like the sun coming from behind a huge cloud as I relive that fateful day when the fish of my dad's dreams drilled the bait and the Ol man won the only battle he ever had with a Musky.

You have to love it, when a plan comes together

Capt Jim's Classic 1000 Islands Boat, the "No Problem"
resting at ease in the Clayton NY Antique Boat Museum

2

My Fishing Partner:

I'M VERY BLESSED. My friends will tell you I am and even strangers will tell you the same. Especially if they have just met me for only a few moments while fishing on a river or stream simply because they witnessed my Fishing Partner in action. My fishing partner in a few short years developed into a fully functional, highly successful fresh and salt water fly fishing angler.

My fishing partner is small in stature standing 5' 3" inches, but can execute long tight loops across a river, or bone fish flat as if SHE had been doing it since she could walk. The pretty blonde ponytail poking out of her fishing cap is a dead giveaway for anglers who fish around us often, and she's become so popular she holds court with other anglers who always seem to have time to stop by and chat with her.

My wife Lindsay wanted to learn how to fly fish and so we got started and in a few years has landed 100's of trout and salmon, bass, blue gills, along with bonefish, stripers, Albies, Permit and Tarpon. I've been in this game of sport fishing for nearly 50 years and have never experienced an anglers rise to excellence as fast as Lindsay. Yeah it sounds very biased but I can bring dozens of testimonies to the witness stand to corroborate my story.

A while ago we were fishing a small free stone creek in North central PA. She had never been on this water before. We dropped in by a nice bridge early evening and the trout were just starting to find emergers and a few duns on the surface. I immediately knew these fish were not going to be easy and told her so. She has a relentless sense of determination and wanted to try but heck it was only 6:30 PM. I said let's wait until they get a little less selective namely let's wait till near dark. However she decided to try it for a while. At one point a local angler walked up and asked her how she was making out. "Not too well yet"...to which he clearly stated..."Don't waste" your time... they can't be caught even at dark. They've seen it all"....

Lindsay smiled at the gentleman which unbeknownst to him had pretty much shoveled a half ton of coal into her boiler because now he had raised the stakes. "CAN'T BE DONE...CAN'T BE CAUGHT. We moved off to a nice little run down stream to where I took two nice browns on a BWO while Lind's had yet to catch a fish. Just as we are about to leave a fish flashes the surface in the tumbling riffle and she immediately fires a cast that way and sure enough, up he comes and eats her fly. Decent rainbow that puts on a nice little acrobatic show. Now it's about 8 PM still not stupid fish time but she wants at the bridge again.

We wander back up nobody fishing there, yet plenty of people around...BUT NOT THERE...not at the spot where they say it can't happen. She figures out the right side of the bridge has a slightly better flow then the left and settles in fishing her Slate Drake down that seam. Two minutes in, she hooks up but drops the fish. Looked like another rainbow. Minutes later she has a 15 inch rainbow doing cartwheels across the pool and brings it to hand. 10 casts later the fish's twin shows up to play with her. Now a few people are gathering up on the bridge to watch. At dusk she decides to vanquish ALL the bridge demons and fish the hardly flowing left side. Our two fishing partners show up just in time to see her little 7 FT 4WT doubled over with the largest fish of the trip which hasn't showed itself but is burrowing deep in the run. I figure it to be a nice brown and finally see the shadow and it's all of 18 inches and wide.

She finally slides the fish in my net and to our amazement it's a big

Brookie, biggest one I've ever seen in countless trips to this area. She isn't arrogant, she isn't cocky, just confident. The word "Can't" isn't in her vocabulary yet she's humble and appreciates these difficult fish and our friends who have seen this before I think now expect it of her. With a flash light walk back to the truck she's pleased with herself, but not ready to shoot off fireworks and yell hooray. She nuzzles up close in the cab with me and says that glass of wine back at the B&B is going to taste extra good tonight.

Honey I Can't Hear The Birds Singing

As more women come to fly fishing, there is now many situations where women can be taught by other women, and certainly men who aren't their husbands or boyfriends. And that is the most significant statement here. Most women do not want to learn the sport of fly fishing from their significant others. Which is one of the main reasons for the past decade my Fly Fishing now Licensed Guide wife Lindsay has run a Trout Unlimited (TU) women's on the water seminar for beginners who want to give the sport a try.

She might have seen the need for such a service after being taught to fly fish by ME! To set the record straight she ASKED me to teach her, so one might say she got what she asked for. I will say that never have I taught someone to fly fish, from casting to catching, fly trying and the strategies on how to catch fish on a fly that learned faster than my wife. There I said it again.

Her second year in, we were past me having to stand next to her, tie on her fly, and tell her what to do. She could wade and fish on her own, pick out her own flies, and she was having some measured success. It's April 4, my Birthday, and we'd always take the day of our birthdays off from work to fish. It's a gray slate day, no color anywhere. It's early spring no green in the trees, the march grasses along the stream are stale brown, with snow remnants still hugging the trail along this pretty stream.

Water condition was perfect. Slightly stained but a good flow height that creates much more holding water. We pull up to the walk in, and there are no other cars or anglers at this spot. The wind is biting with tiny darts of freezing rain pricking our faces. We gear up wearing our winter wear and start walking into the runs. Lindsay's main goal is for me to catch a nice lake run Brown Trout or Steelhead. Whenever we fish together I'm truly not content until she has caught a fish as well.

But since it's my Birthday, she gives me honors to pick the best slot, and she'd fish nearby or follow me down river. We were on a stream that I grew up fishing, to say I knew every rock, run and slot in this section of river would be an understatement. I find a good lie that I'm confident holds fish, and sure enough 15 minutes into our day, I have two pretty drop back Brown Trout to the net. My day has been made. Once Lind's catches a fish, we can be in a diner 10 minutes away, enjoying a hot cup of coffee, and some pancakes.

"Ok honey, why don't you step into this spot, I'm sure there are more fish in this run". Lind's also wants to catch a fish or two, and she knows my Birthday would be complete if we both netted a nice big lake run trout. I'm now standing on the bank and I give her the coordinates on where to land her fly so it would swing into the strike zone. She makes the first couple casts, pretty much nowhere near I had directed her to. Figured she just had to get her bearings. About the fifth cast to the wrong slot, I stepped in close and inches from her left ear, pointing to where she needs to cast. Again off target...I'm in close again..."No honey, just upstream right in by that bush"....my words you could see them like a cartoon bubble in a comic book were hanging over her, and she burst the bubble wide open, turned to me with the same look in her eyes as Regan had in the Exorcist when she told the priest to Fuck off.

"I CAN'T HEAR THE BIRDS SINGING DAVE". Which if you think about it, was a very nice way of saying "**Dave shut the fuck up and leave me alone**". WOOOOOOW OK OK I get it, and I stepped away and went down stream. Not sure if she ever made the right cast to get to the fish, but after a few minutes she stepped away and we headed to the next likely spot.

Now even at this point in Lindsay's fly fishing career, she was way ahead of the curve on reading water. She wasn't familiar with this particular section of the stream, so as I hiked ahead of her to make sure I gave her enough room to hear the birds singing, even though it was so nasty out there wasn't a bird within miles puckering up with a pretty morning song. She yelled out, where do you think I should fish in this run? **Oh did I hear that right??....She was asking for my help?**

Now I'm much older and mature than I used to be, so if I wanted to end my Birthday say with some romantic loving, I wasn't going to be an asshole and tell her to figure it out herself, even though I had approached that thought. I doubled back and looked over the run. "I'd come up to the head of this run, make a cast (and I pointed to the spot with my rod), and then to NOT encroach her space started to walk away. I could see in my peripheral vision she was making the cast. I continued down the trail, when I heard a distinctive splash. I spun around to see my girl tight to a beautiful fish. Figured it was a Steelhead since it came three feet out of the water, but as she deftly swung the fish to the beach, it was a nice Brownie.

Of course Lindsay had a huge smile on her face, kind of in-between "told you I could do this....but hey thank you". She had this goofy winter ski hat on her head, and I lifted it off her head for the picture of my pretty girl and her fish. This was back in the days we still shot film and had to get it processed and printed. When we got the pictures back she looked like Helga of the Swedish Fly Fishing team, her pretty blonde hair all astray.

In her seminars, she teaches the girls that if their significant others are pestering them too much while fishing, Toss the ol' "I CAN'T HEAR THE BIRDS SINGING line to back them down.

*Lindsay with a pretty lake run Brown Trout smiling
because she can hear "The Birds Singing"*

HEY LADY DON'T YOU HAVE SOME SHOPPING TO DO!

Today it's much more common to see lady anglers along the tributaries. Orvis has their 50/50 program going to where they are trying to encourage more women into the sport of fly fishing in hopes there will be an equal balance of men and women fishing our rivers. Of course it's a marketing ploy for them, but most fly fishing gear and tackle companies are on the same band wagon. Personally I love to see more women on the water. Seems to me the boys behave better in the presence of female anglers.

Flash back about 10 years ago when lady anglers were not the norm, Lind's and I were fishing for Steelhead on a local trib about an hour from our house. This river is well known for solid runs of Brown and Rainbow/Steelhead trout from Lake Ontario. It was spring and fish were migrating in from the lake. This day we were having better than average success fishing some wet flies and nymphs through some good holding water. I state this, because the men fishing nearby were NOT having even moderate success. Lind's cast into the top of a run, and suddenly her arm was lit up with a heavy fish, much bigger then the cookie cutter four to six pound bows we had been catching. This fish decided to take center stage in the run, and the other men did the right thing by taking their lines out of the water to give Lindsay room to fight this fine specimen. The fish launched out of the water and showed itself, and now it was evident that we were dealing with a trophy fish of possibly 14 or 15 pounds.

The fish left the run and screamed downstream, Lind's calmly in pursuit keeping a tight line to her prize. About 30 yards down range from where she started she slid a tired big hen into the net. We knelt in the water with the fish for several minutes reviving her. Triumphant we marched up stream to reset the game. However one of the "Gentlemen" who had seen enough of the Dave and Lindsay show, had moved into the slot she was fishing. Lind's politely asked if she could step back in as she was fishing there. The guy snapped at her, "Well you're not fishing here anymore."

Unfazed, Lindsay moved up to where this sportsman had been beating the water to a froth with no success. It wasn't five minutes later, that she hooked another dime bright hen of 10 plus pounds and as the fish sped down stream with her fly in its jaw, Lindsay had to excuse herself as she danced past the "Gentlemen" who had taken her slot…."excuse me sir", I need to get around you," dazed and confused he stepped aside, and she landed the fish a few paces below him.

The guys across the river I guess had seen enough of this pretty blonde just dialed in on the bite, and a guy finally yelled out at the top of his lungs **"Hey Lady, don't you have some shopping to do, or go get your nails done"**. We both chuckled…broke down our rods since we didn't want to overstay our welcome with regards to the fish, and I answered, "We're done, we'll let you guys have a chance". And waded out of the water and off to a hot lunch and cold brew.

THE GOLDEN GUIDE:

I spent nearly 20 years guiding anglers and enjoyed it "Most" of the time. About 15 years ago, I sold my business, and not because I didn't want to guide any more, but rather my youngest daughter Brittany who was an accomplished athlete was on some elite premier teams playing basketball and soccer and traveling around the Northeast, and I wasn't going to miss that. That lasted about nine years, and while I wasn't guiding I instead started traveling when not chasing Britt to fish places I always dreamt of .

My lovely wife Lindsay was traveling with me and learning as mentioned earlier at a very fast pace. Several years ago I began volunteering and working for Project Healing Waters. In the spring of 2011, PHW had a woman soldier who wanted to come to an event. This soldier had been through some really rough times overseas, and had been severely injured. The two days Lindsay spent with her were amazing, to the point that one of the soldiers in command of the event took time to seek her out and warmly thank her for the care she provided this veteran.

Now it was Nov. and the second PHW event was coming up. PHW invited Lindsay to help out once again even though they didn't have any women anglers this time. Lind's has a heart that is very special and has spent a life time of caring and sharing herself with those in need. So she jumped at the chance to join us for some Steelhead fishing.

The night before the first day of fishing, the guides meet the soldiers in a social setting. We share a meal, make some connections and tie flies for the next day. Lindsay is a wonderful fly tier, and it didn't take but about 10 minutes and she had two or three soldiers looking over her shoulder while she showed them a hot steelhead pattern and then traded places with them so they could learn to tie it as well.

Day one of the event started out at about 26 degrees. The Sun was bright, and the weatherman promised we'd end up with a day in the mid 40's. We were a long way from there. Generally PHW likes to have these events where they can find quiet water for the Wounded Warriors. The Salmon River in New York State up at the NYS Department of Environmental Conservation (DEC) hatchery water was the perfect place. About a mile of easily wadable water, secluded from the general public. The way the Salmon River and the hatchery are laid out is, the trout and salmon return to spawn in the river, and many of them swim up a small feeder stream right into the fish way ladders that lead them into the hatchery. However the main river runs past the hatchery and goes another couple miles upriver where there is also natural spawning grounds. This was Nov, the last remaining King salmon were still around, including some fairly fresh Coho salmon, and the treasure of this river in the fall, dime bright steelhead who traditionally ascend the river to gorge themselves on the billions of salmon eggs along the stream bottom.

So we had un-pressured water to fish for the Vets. First order of business is for the organizers to assign soldiers with a guide. Those of us that have been volunteering for a while are well known to the event leaders and often if we have a strength that can be matched to a Vets weakness, they'll put us together. I was matched with Stevie, a Sergeant from Texas who is stationed at Fort Drum in the 10th Mountain Division. Stevie had very little experience with a fly rod, and I'm known to be pretty good at teaching newbie's to cast.

Everybody got matched, and it was much like your old neighborhood days picking teams. "I'll take Jimmy, OK I'll take Billy" This went on for the first 11 soldiers, and 11 guides. And nobody, coordinators or vets picked Lindsay. There was only one Vet left a young sturdy looking soldier named David Ira Strouse. He went by Ira, and so Lind's stepped up and stuck her hand out and gave Ira a warm but firm handshake. I just smiled to myself. Only a couple of the guides knew Lindsay, most didn't know her from Adam or in this case Eve.

Lindsay is fully functional on her own, but we decided to team up with our friend Charlie and the three of us grab some water and get these guys started. Lindsay had Ira in the tail out of this nice pool, and she had fish milling around in the fast water just below where Charlie and I were setup with our Vets. Within the first hour all three of us had taken pictures of our soldiers with landed fish, both steelhead and pretty Coho salmon. Stevie and I decided to move up river a bit and Lindsay stayed low. I didn't see her and Ira until the end of the first day.

This is how the story was told. While Ira had successfully caught and Lindsay netted a couple Coho salmon and a small steelhead, he told her he had never caught a Brown trout. He's always wanted to catch a Brown. Now I have to say while the Salmon river has a decent population of brown trout, it's not like you can easily target them, especially when behind every rock there is a spawned out king, Coho or just arrived steelhead. The property in which we were bound to had mostly fast water, plunge pools, a few holding pools that were jammed with dying kings. There was the very last tail out in this section that wasn't too fast. Lindsay is an experienced Great Lakes Brown trout fly fisher, so she said to Ira. Our best shot at a brown trout is down there. Pointing to a run, that by the way they could only fish from the other side of the river. This meant trying to get across a very slippery fairly heavy current, climb along some rocks, drop down into the water with big boulders at your back and swing a streamer, wet fly or nymph through the tail out.

Lind's wasn't sure she could cross in this water level, but told Ira if he was willing to give it a try she'd go for it. Ira is a soldier, so hesitating he wasn't. Arm in arm they crossed together and slowly made their way to the other side. Climbed up and then down the boulders, and finally arrived in a spot that nobody had fished yet. Lindsay perfected a timeless fly called a Springs Wiggler. It's a wet fly/nymph in sizes 6,8, and 10 that works well for browns and steelhead. Ira asked what fly she wanted him to try and she opened her box and tied on a chartreuse wiggler.

Lindsay told me later, she was just reaching, she had no idea if there were any brown trout within 10 miles of us, but reading the water and looking at the flow, if there was one around, it would probably be in here. Ira rolled out a cast....the fly swung downstream, he felt a take and set the hook. The water boiled, and the fish stayed down and dogged towards the bottom, Lind's said she figured another Coho. As they became stale they still fight hard but pretty much stopped all the aerial shows. Ira stayed tight to the fish, and it was a decent size fish. Lindsay instructed him to climb back up on the rocks to be able to swing it into her. She by the way had to leave the net behind, for the group that was fishing next to her to use back up stream, so she had to tail this fish. Finally the fish came into view, and they both gasped and looked at each other in amazement, it was in fact a nice big fully colored up yellow/orange bellied 7 to 8 pound BROWN TROUT. Ira couldn't believe it. Lindsay up to her waist (mostly because she's a tiny 5'3") now had to not screw this up and grab this fish. Ira of course had to have a picture with his very first ever trophy brown trout.

Ira swung the fish to Lindsay, and she deftly tailed the fish and cradles it under her other hand. Ira is sitting up on the rocks as giddy as a little kid on Christmas morning when Lindsay breaks his trance and says "IRA get down here and grab your fish so I can take a picture". Laughing, the two of them gather themselves, and Ira cradles his prize. Lind's snaps the pics and the fish is released...high fives, hugs are exchanged, and just as if Ira simply had to order up what fish he wanted to catch next, his guide delivered.

At the end of the first day stories were running rampant. Ira and Lindsay were the last two to arrive. They were the furthest downstream. The banter had receded to a gentile roar when the two of them rolled into the parking lot. Ira with his arms raised yelled out to the crowd...."I...Have ...THE GOLDEN GUIDE" His tally at the end of the day was nearly 10 fish landed, and he had hit the Salmon River slam, landing three different species of fish, Steelhead, Coho's and his first ever Brown Trout.

There is no score keeping at these events except the soldiers are very competitive, but no one was arguing the fact, that the last guide picked in the draft turned out to be the Super Bowl MVP.....the Golden of All Guides. Her guy caught so many fish, the soldiers changed his name from Ira....to FLYRA.

3

Fat Albert & "MEDIUM" Lodging

NOT TOO LONG ago two very dear friends and I decided to embark on an adventure to Connecticut to fish for False Albacore tuna. Now to get started my friend Charlie is a gentleman of distinguished background. A PHD in phycology he is the former VP at the college I graduated from although he wasn't there when I was. Chas is about 12 years my senior, a veteran, and in simplest terms one hell of a fantastic guy to hang out with.

My first audience with Charlie happened many years ago. I was fishing the famed Salmon River in New York State on a piece of water called the Douglaston Salmon Run (DSR) down low in the Meadow section. It was early Sept. on a Sunday afternoon and I was all alone on this piece of water. My game was hoping to find a few early run Chinook Salmon out of Lake Ontario. The Meadow hole was the first good resting place out of the estuary about a half click up stream. I was swinging a 14 foot two handed rod with a large streamer in hopes that an early arrival would become a player and crack this fly. It was 3 PM, I had fruitlessly fished through this run a few times and was stepping back up to start again after the next fly change. Half way down I get the grab that every swinger fishes for. That lighting "Jolt' up through my arm to my brain and it was on. A pure silver King rolled up to the surface to find out what just bit her back in the lower jaw. The power of this fresh fish was daunting as she dashed up stream and then down. Plenty of side pressure had her near my boot laces twice but each time she scrambled off as I jostled with the 14 foot stick to try and get my hands on her tail. I noticed in my peripheral vision a guy standing there watching me. On the third round the big silver hen delivered the knock-out punch and escaped fly in her jaw unfortunately.

I had been at it all day and leaned against the bank mesmerized half dazed, happy yet pissed off that I lost the one take I'd had all day when a voice broke my trance. It was Charlie and he said..."Thought you had that fish whipped". "Me to" I knew who Charlie was because we had a mutual friend yet he and I had never actually met. Heard stories about each other through our mutual friend but this was our initial greeting. It was fitting as we've shared some wonderful days on rivers since then.

Charlie and I would fish the Salmon river together, some tribs near my neck of the woods and even the famed Soo Rapids but this story is about Charlie introducing me to "Little Tunny". Charlie told stories of the False Albacore Tuna fishing in Long Island sound out of Watch Hill Rhode Island. He had been several times and offered that on a fly rod, few fish were more challenging for sheer power and speed.

I tend to be the planner scheduler for our adventures the past couple years so I set up a two day outing with a guide that Charlie introduced Lindsay and I to who had taken us striper fishing. This story is going to take a couple of detours twists and turns so stay with me.

I'm the kind of guy who likes to connect several dots together when going fishing. Our Tuna trip was for the last two days of Sept. I live the farthest west of our Stonington Connecticut destination, our mutual friend, renown distance running athlete and highly attributed Catskill Museum Hall Of Fame Fly Fishing guide Fran Verdoliva near the Salmon River and Charlie living just east of Fran. So it made sense since late Sept. is great fishing on the Salmon river for Salmon and Trout, I'd go a day early, fish the river, then pick the boys up and we'd head to the Sound.

Our guided trips were for Tuesday and Wed. of that week...I decided to go early Sunday, fish the river all day, stay with Fran Sunday night fish a couple hours Monday morning then off to get Charlie in New Woodstock . (yeah it's out in the middle of NO WHERE). I left home at 4 AM on Sunday, as I hurried out the door just before kissing my bride good-bye, I noticed three bananas in the fruit dish. Knowing Lindsay isn't a big Banana fan I decided to grab them to snack on during the day since I'll be gone for four days

I arrive at the Salmon River, it's raining and there are a ton of people around but I find a slot to fish and there are fish moving up through mostly Coho's. I'm swinging wet flies and streamers... nothing! Turn to nymphing , and indicator fishing, still nothing not a single take. Guys around me are catching a few fish nobody is really into them for the amount of fish around. I'm frustrated yet determined and I stay with it until I look at my watch realizing I've fished since 7 AM it's now 3:30 without a break. I had moved to several different slots in the river, fished to countless passing fish and not a single grab.

I'm due at Fran's for dinner so I break down in the rain beaten and wet, I stumble back to my truck. The first thing I see laying on the seat is the three bananas I brought from home. Now being a former Charter Boat Capt. with over 20 years of service on Lake Ontario, I know that a Banana is never welcome on a boat in the case of fishing. Fishing success goes into the toilet let alone the historical reasons not to have bananas on your boat which is bad things happen to you and your vessel. I've threatened my Charter clients that I'd leave them at the dock if they tried to bring a banana on my boat.

So I'm sitting there eyeing the bananas. I start to laugh, could it be the same curse is for a river angler if in possession of said cursed fruit? Not taking any chances and with a short window to fish on Monday and then the Albi trip, I sat there soaking wet actually hungry since I hadn't eaten a thing all day and choked down all three bananas.

Next morning Fran who is the Salmon River Program Coordinator and Special Assistant for New York State Department of Environmental Conservation (DEC) had to clean up some paper work till noon and then we'd hit the trail. I dropped Fran off at the Salmon River hatchery in Altmar NY and since I was close by the Upper Fly Fishing only zone, decided to take a ride over there fully expecting the place to be overrun with people. This little mile and a half piece of water is a Steelheader's princess. Classic fly fishing water with runs riffles and pools. You can't see how many cars are in the parking lot until you actually hit the entrance. I wheeled my F150 into the gravel entrance to the spooky realization there was NO BODY else there. Not a single car. Now it was 8:30 AM so conceivably anglers could have been in here at day break and left already because the fishing was off.

Either way I was getting excited, one of the most treasured spots in here is a slick pool that dumps into a long white water run with plenty of seams and current breaks to hold fish. The pool looks like a puddle of maple syrup. It's moving with nary a ripple on the water's surface. I walk up in there and the bank is about 8 feet high off the water so you have to scramble down a washout. Because the pool is so slick you have to do it carefully and quietly so as not to spook the fish. I ease down in the water and slowly make my way to the top of the pool. First order of the day is to swing a streamer in hopes of getting the tug that is the drug of all swingers.

I was using my Sage 8110 switch rod with a Scandi head. Water was fairly low and I didn't envision needing any weight other than the cone head fly I decided to start with. Cast step, cast step. On the third cast I felt a double grab like the fish dropped the fly then caught it, line tightened I raised the Sage, sank the steel and the surface bubbled with a pretty heavy fish. It wasn't jumping or running hard, thought stale Coho or nice brown trout. Walked down below the fish who had decided to run to the other side of the pool and in minutes I was beaching a cinnamon colored brown trout in the 10 pound class, his bleach white mouth agape with my cone head fly in his lower jaw.

Shook my head and started to smile maybe it WAS the bananas. Reset to the top of the pool and started to step cast again. At the tail, the pool runs to a sharp V to where it dumps into the froth below and I notice the water is very nervous. I see some ripples moving around down there pushing the syrupy water upstream in the wrong direction. But, I stay calm and cast by cast move within swinging distance of the V. Figured a pod of Coho's or maybe a pair of King Salmon were staging at the tail.

Made the long cast, the fly swung down to the Apex and I got the pull that is the addiction lurching my whole right side forward. I didn't need to raise the rod as the fish buried the tip almost into the water. My minds score board lit up "King Salmon" with that kind of power ....ANNNNNNT...the sound of the game show buzzer rang in my head however as a silver missile launched four feet in the air, a jaw dropping moment realizing this fish was a bright chrome steelhead of 14 or 15 pounds.

I scrambled over the rough bottom of boulders that are every size imaginable to get below this beast because if she hit that fast water way ahead of me we'd either be dancing for the next quarter mile or she'd pull free. I know this hole and was able to skip below the fish two more great leaps and I was below her putting side pressure to the downstream direction, forcing her up into the white froth trying to run away from the pressure. We ended the fight much quicker with me below her. She lay glistening in a few inches of water easily 15 pounds of fresh steel. What a comeback I had just staged, yesterday not a single take today in the first 30 minutes two wonderful fish. I released the hen looked over my shoulder and the pool had four new members standing in it tossing flies, game over. I wandered about a half mile down river to fish the tail of another great run with only one guy at the head and he invited me to fish the tail. On the very first cast...BANG... my second steelhead of the day this one about six or seven pounds also mint dime bright silver.

IT WAS THE BANANA'S....it had to be.

And now finally on to Connecticut. Fran and I left the hatchery about 1 PM, got to Charlies and hour later to where his wife Judy greeted us with a fresh loaf of hot brown bread and a bean soup. A perfect and delicious meal to get us on the road.

The drive to Stonington was enjoyable with lots of banter but prior to departure I had made a last second call to our guide because the weather forecast looked doubtful. Capt. Steve said it looked like we'd have a window both Tuesday and Wednesday to get out so we hit the trail. In the back of our minds we watched the weather, checked forecasts along the way on our phones and at approximately 9 PM pulled into the parking lot of the motel. The pictures on the internet looked delightful. Our guide Steve had recommended it as a no frills but OK place to stay for a fishing trip. Not a place to bring the wife or significant other but for fishermen it was perfect.

Charlie and I walked in....I knew the place was run by people of Middle Eastern decent. The office was empty except for the distinct smell of "curry" when this young kid walks in and smiles at me. I say "I have a reservation and I'd like to check in". He just smiles and starts to speak in his native tongue. I worked internationally and was used to figuring out how to communicate with others who didn't speak the Kings English, so I'm calm, slow down and start to gesture that we want a key and a room to stay the night. This young kid seemed to be taking pleasure in the fact that he's on the Motel Key side of the desk and I'm not, and he can't seem to understand why I'm there. I calmly ask if anyone is around who speaks English. The kid starts yelling as if I was trying to steal the cash register. The door swings open again and an older gentleman walks in. He starts to get excited as if we are there to rob them, still calm I ask do you speak English, he says **"Medium"**... speaks medium English. I look at Charlie and probably about now I'm not as calm as I think I am retelling this story so I recite my opening again, my name and I have reservations.....this guy who appears to be grandpa...is LOST....has no fucking idea...what I'm trying to say....and then another young guy comes in...accompanied by what was probably grandma....in her nightgown...all yapping away excitedly in their native tongue...all trying to dial the phone. My temper is raising, **and Charlie the true blue friend he is... is like the boiler tech in the engine room of a big ship...he's shoveling coal into my boiler....just nudging me on.....**

And it worked, these folks can't transpose the number fucking 8 from the piece of paper they are holding to pushing the number 8 on the phone to call whoever they are trying to call, which I assume is maybe the one person in all of Connecticut that can speak what ever language they are jabbering and English but we aren't going to be able to speak to that person because this crew can't dial the fucking phone. They're all yelling and talking loud and now Charlie who is much more refined then I is egging me on.

All I can see in my mind's eye is the Movie Scent of A Women where Al Pacino is sitting at a table on the stage at the Baird School while the faculty is holding a trial of his friend **"Charlie"**...and he slams his fist on the table...and says, "I'd like to TAKE A FLAME THROWER TO THIS PLACE". That was me, that's where I was at.....six hours on the road since 3 PM, up since about 5:30 AM that day it's pouring outside we can't speak to the four people who have the keys to the motel and we have no other place to stay.

Finally the second young kid gets someone on the phone and in two minutes the fifth person of this clan is marching in the door with his Shell Mini Mart jacket on and hands me the key to room 10. Ahhhh...but now I'm wise to where I am with all the commotion going on. I tell Mini Mart Man I want to see the room first. So Charlie and I walk down to good ol' room 10. We unlock the door and a tidal wave of mold and mildew wishes over us. We turn on the light and realize it's not a coincidence there isn't ONE other person staying at this place on this Monday night, not one car in the lot and the last time this room was rented might have been in the 1950's.

My first new friend who greeted me in the office had followed us down to the room figuring we were all set. He was ready to scramble back to the office and tell his clan, "Hey the Gringo's bought it...we are going to make some money here" But NO, I told him no thanks we have decided to go elsewhere in very broken "MEDIUM" English he offered us two more keys to check out rooms but we declined and got back in the car. This place was just around the corner from Capt. Steve's boat. So we drove around in the dark, in a deluge and found two other places along the route neither looked much better. So we headed 10 minutes down the road to Mystic CT and found the friendly sign of a Howard Johnson's that was very modern very clean had a very nice young lady at the desk...WHO SPOKE GREAT ENGLISH.

To brighten the night there was a steak and micro beer joint across the road that served until midnight. Seeing it was pushing 11 PM, we dumped our gear in the room and finally slumped into some comfortable chairs with cold micro-brews and a hot meal....And every other word out of Charlies ball busting mouth .... was MEDIUM!

Next morning rain had stopped but the wind was on the verge of blowing a gale once the clouds moved out and was replaced by clear skies. We grabbed some coffee and a quick hot breakfast sandwich and got to the boat before 6 AM. Capt. Steve had the boat ready and while he wasn't overly certain the weather would cooperate we were going to make a run for it. We headed out to Watch Hill and as we turned out into the open water of LI Sound we were met with an abrupt get your attention chop that of course got more of your attention as we steamed to the fishing grounds. Open center console in four footers up on the bow...trying to fly cast...is all about being athletic. I was using a 425 grain rig since there wasn't any birds diving the grounds. Casting and reloading that rig in this chop was first and foremost an exercise to not put the fly in your ear lobe.

About 20 minutes of that dance and Capt. Steve said we'd run up the river to see if we can find any bass . By then the Sun was breaking out and as expected the wind speed went from the low 20's to about mid 30's with gusts to 40. The boat ride up the river was lovely. Charlie and I are boat buffs and we loved looking at all the fishing rigs, some classic's but no birds no bass no Albies.....back to the dock.

Checked the weather for Wednesday. Steve still thought there might be a window of opportunity. Hell we were already here, although my mind drifted back to the salmon river where if we left now I could be swinging to fresh steel at daybreak on Wednesday.

We decided to sit it out at the shore, so we spent the day rambling around Rhode Island and Connecticut stopping in some seafood joints for fresh vitals. Charlie has a host of friends he fishes salt water with that all live down in this area. For the rest of the day his phone is ringing with his buddies telling him some beaches to hit in hopes of finding some water that isn't at tidal wave stage rolling onto the sand. We are driving all over the place on directions from guys who I don't really know. I appreciate their efforts but bottom line the wind was at 30 knots against the shore EVERYWHERE.

Charlie's been to all kinds of places in this area on too many fishing trips to count. Yet he really doesn't know where anything is. He'd been talking about this little joint for two days that we had to get to, but couldn't remember exactly how to get there. To his credit yet lack of total recall he got us within a couple blocks of this neat little bar restaurant and we luckily guessed the right turn at the right time and pulled in the parking lot.

We strolled in, it was quaint complete with an older gentleman bar tender with a white apron on kind like Coach in the TV show Cheers. We decided to sit and eat at the bar. The food was great and banter between us and the other patrons was fun. What wasn't fun is the barkeep knowing of our plight to fish in the morning had put the weather channel up and it was ugly. NO way were we going to get out. We'll show up at Steve's boat get the bad news, hit the road and be home around noon on the Salmon River by about 2 PM .and maybe get into a trout or salmon before dark. I always and I mean always, have plan "B" in my hip pocket.

Up at five bells on Wednesday Sept. 30. Last day of Sept, car was packed, rods still rigged from the day before and off we went. The stop at Duncan Doughnuts for coffee and a hot sausage biscuit and down to the boat. We jump out and Steve has just arrived. He walks up to us, I'm waiting to hear the …."Sorry boys…just isn't going to happen"…but instead Steve says he jumped on the UCONN science site that has access to weather buoys out in the sound and the winds are down under five knots right now it's calm out there let's go.

Shocked….and for sure the wind isn't blowing at the dock but what kind of residual waves are awaiting us once we break the bay out to the sound. Hmmm not to bad and this time we are headed in the opposite direction since the wind and waves are down we're running in the later predicted up wind direction to have a nicer ride back when she starts to kick up. We run for about 20 minutes and ease into a bay. No birds around so Steve directs a couple of us to blind cast this area. Steve like most good guides, works in tandem with another very well know skipper out of his marina, and on about my fourth cast Steve is on the cell phone and excitedly yells get your lines in...we got the "Come On" call from the other boat. It's on at the Race. I look at Charlie, I see the gleam in his eyes, and he mouths "Race Lighthouse"

Lines in, rods in the holders, Capt. Steve has the big Merc roaring to life, we are battened down and out of the hole in a flash. Still not very bumpy so we can cruise along at a good clip holding onto our hats, even screwed on catcher style the back draft was almost shooting the cap off your dome.

We glide into the rip and the birds are in a frenzy. One eye to the water will tell you why. Mouths are snapping at the surface and little fish are leaping all over the place. Charlie has been here before and he invites Fran and I to take first shot at the blitz. Now by big blitz standards, this isn't huge or so I'm told but it's easy to see where the fish are. We slide alongside some working birds, I see some splashes, make a 40 foot cast to cover the fish get the 10 weight low to the water and start a fast strip. Not counting, don't know if it was the third or fourth school I tossed to, but most likely in the first five minutes of fishing, I who was ready for the grab simply from the coaching I get from Chas...It happens. ....and it's still not what I expected. More like a thug grabbing you by the collar from behind. Sudden and VIOLENT like a head on collision, I strip set hard and before I could raise my rod, the tip is buried in the salty water and my Tibor is spinning like a pinwheel in a hurricane with 3 quarters set of drag pressure and this fish is off to the races. You can't teach speed and power, many before me have experienced this for those that never have....if you ever do...it will be burned into your memory forever. Now I've caught Yellowfin tuna trolling and at the end of the fight I've been through the death spiral or pinwheel but an eight pound Albie on a 10 weight fly rod swimming under the boat is a tug of war with what seems like a truck.

Finally ….The fish is in the boat, high fives and back slaps quick pictures and little Tunny is back in the water. Charlie is smiling and looking at me, and he's getting the reaction he expected I'm sure. One of amazement and pure joy because we love hard fighting fish from pound and a half blue gills to trout and salmon, bone fish and tarpon and now the Albie.

Mr Fat Albert. The four fastest fish that swims on the planet.

I know what it feels like to open a new fishing door for a friend or in the past as a Charter Boat Captain. To be with them as they experience something for the first time that dazzles them and makes a lasting impression. This was one of those moments. Many Albies would hit the deck that day with another 5 or 6 that got away. The second fish took me a full 35 minutes to land and I leaned on that 10 weight as hard as I ever have. I lost a fish around a buoy that was

close to 200 yards away simply because I thought I could turn him before he got there and didn't tell Capt. Steve we needed to chase the
fish. I didn't make that mistake again. Thanks to Charlie, this was not
a MEDIUM experience.

Charlie ("Chas") and Capt. Steve Burnett

4

My First Time (in Alaska)

IT WAS RAINING sideways, and the wind was stiff out of the west. The smell of gasoline and oil awakened my senses as the scarlet red De-Havilland Beaver chugged up the river. This classic bush plane rattled and shook in the face of the stormy weather. But she never wavered when Gary finally threw the throttle forward pulled back on the yoke and she launched herself up into the wind her engine roaring with ear splitting power. THIS WAS ALASKA! I like so many first timers before me sat mesmerized craning my neck from the close quarters of the Beaver in search of wild life through the jack pines below. At 600 feet you can see into the water and I found myself fumbling in my pack for my polarized fishing glasses so I could peruse every pond and stream for fish.

With the wind raging at 35 knots our pilot Gary had to spiral down to the Alagnak River. We made three swings around the target like a flock or weary mallards looking to set down in the middle of a decoy spread. We touched down and to my amazement fish scooted out from under the plane everywhere. A moment before I'd talked myself into actually seeing some dark greenish brown backs from 200 foot, and now I knew I actually did. I saw red flashes on the fish as they scrambled away from the pontoons of the Beaver. I turned to Woody and Rob, two of my new fishing companions for the week, and told them I had just seen a pod of rainbows run from the hole we landed in.

An hour later after meeting the head guide Trapper Young in camp, having a nice lunch of sandwiches and hot broccoli soup, I laced up my new never been fished before 6 weight 10 foot Sage RPL+. Trapper selected a pink marabou fly imitation. It wouldn't have been my first choice even though I had done my homework and realized that pink marabou was a hot pattern in Alaska. But hey! Don't second guess the head guide on the very first day.

We ran back down river to the hole we had landed in. I cranked up the fly and delivered a crisp 50 foot cast into the seam of the flow. My third strip as the fly swung into the thick water was stopped suddenly and on instinct, I yanked the fly line with my stripping hand, and lifted the rod sharply. The very first fish hooked on this stick was a four pound hen pink salmon with small black spots and scarlet coloring along her flanks. Her brown and white undersides made a distinct impression in my mind to a fish I was seeing for the very first time in real life. The 10 footer danced in my hand as the fish leaped and splashed about. Jody my guide for the afternoon slipped the fish free from the hook and in the drizzle, and the cold, and wild background of the tundra and mountains, I broke into a very silly smile. Nine months of planning, 14 hours of traveling from the east coast, and on my first cast, I catch a fish that I've never caught before...or will EVER catch back in western New York. She fought like a tiger, she was beautiful. In two and a half hours I managed to release 20 or so pinks. Many real nice male humpys that to some might look a little grotesque but to me were just another amazing piece of the splendid wildlife puzzle in Alaska.

It was now that I realized the fish that flew from underneath our landing was a huge school of pinks. After a dozen fish landed I started switching flies to see if it was me having a fantastic day luring fish to the fly, or were the fish so sappy, they'd hit anything. I discovered, if they like the fly, they will jump on it even if it only has a few turns of feathers left. But I did manage to find a couple flies the pinks turned their noses up on. That actually made me feel pretty good. The others in my party were having very good success. Woody Davis and his daughter Connie were keeping Trapper busy releasing fish for them, while Rob was hanging pinks alongside me. I thought it would certainly take me three or four days to catch enough fish to put the rod down and start drinking in the splendor of this wild land. But after a while I found myself taking a break, sitting back and watching the others fish, and admiring the river, the tundra and the mountains.

The Katmai National Park is mostly tundra with some rolling hills and ridges. No dense forests far as the eye can see, but instead scrub and jack pines, with rich grasses. Far off in the distance snowcapped mountains stood guard over this rugged land. Most of the time the cloud cover was too low for us to realize the beauty of those mountains. But on a couple occasions during the week, the summits rose out of the mist enough to realize the beauty of this place. The Alagnak River flows hard and crystal clear from the glacier lakes above down to Bristol Bay. This place is wild, and when I stood on the raise behind camp overlooking the whole valley, I realized I was in overwhelming wilderness. There were never going to be a McDonalds or Burger King, shopping malls or apartment buildings for as far as the eye could see. The only infrastructure was the river itself. The only way in or out was to boat up the river some 60 miles from the Bering Sea, or land a small bush plane in the deeper slots surrounded by gravel bars. Man can get in and out, but you can't order a pizza for delivery.

Monday morning and the wind was howling, about 30 knots. Not a blue print day for fly casting. Today we'd go after two fish that I had really planned this trip around. The leopard spotted rainbows, and the beautiful arctic char. In late August with five different species of salmon in the river depositing their rich eggs into the gravel bottoms, wolf packs of rainbows, char and grayling setup camp behind the spawners to dine or maybe a better term gorge themselves on salmon roe. Drifting down river, the game was to spot spawning kings and place egg pattern flies into the flow behind them to the hungry glutinous trout. In the stiff wind and with the same six weight rod as the day before I found myself struggling a little to get the right drift. With a little instruction from Outfitter Charlie Summerville, I started making the proper presentations and began to consistently hook bows, char and grayling. Even the smaller 10 to 12 inch trout were hefty due to the fine dining available in the river. Char with olive green backs, big pink spots and white tipped fins, grayling in the two to three pound range with that cream colored iridescence along their flanks and the beautiful dorsal fin. Finally the plump leopard spotted rainbows, thick scarlet stripes, and spots from their tails to their noses inhaled our egg flies as we swept down the river.

You're drifting quickly, anywhere from 5 to 7 knots depending on the wind. The proper presentation is to have the egg fly traveling close to the gravel bottom so the fish see it tumbling towards them naturally. With such a quick boat ride, often times the fish would just be on. There were not many light takes during the drift portions of the day. Getting down required a couple split shot on a dropper. Casting shot in a stiff breeze from a moving boat is pretty tricky if you've never done it before. The water is moving too fast for the guide to hold you in the current with the oars. On real windy days like this day, Charlie opted to use the big outboard to hold us in position a few times. The general tactic is to use the oars to keep the boat in the middle of the flow. At the end of each drift you pull your line across the front of your body and drop the line on the opposite side of the boat...let the current load the rod and then slingshot it up 45 degrees off the bow of the boat. Throw a quick mend or two upstream to get the fly moving along the gravel bottom. Most times you get the traditional tick tick ticking of shot on the gravel...and a rod ripping strike from a hungry bow, char or grayling. We tore off quite a few fish fighting them in the drag wake of the drift boat. We also landed more then our share of fish, and it was wild to fight them in that fast moving environment. Like I said earlier, these fish were broad shouldered fighters that bored deep in the runs, or leaped three feet in the air after being pinned.

Finishing a morning of drifting through the winding spawning areas, we opted to try and find some silvers (Coho salmon) that were making their way in as the last breed of pacific salmon to enter the river. Charlie took us to a couple of his favorite holes. As we motored up to one such spot, you could see the blue hue in the seam of the river telling you it was loaded with pinks. Now the wind was raging. Rob opted to continue with his spinning rod in the gale. Knowing that I couldn't bust through the breeze with the six weight stick, I un-cased my 14 foot eight weight two handed rod. With a shooting head I was able to cut through the wind tunnel and make decent casts to this pod of fish. One pink after another, some male Humpys that pushed the eight to 10 pound mark attacked my streamers with the recklessness of a herd of wild horses. While we didn't find any silvers in these holes, Rob and I were rewarded with plenty of pinks. Pinks are an interesting fish. First of all they might be the most fly friendly of all the salmon species. The hens fight more like rainbows, with leaps and runs, while the males use that big hump in the current to pump the rod like a big brown trout.

In one frenzy of hookups I handed my Spey rod to Rob, and after he fought a six pound Pink on the long rod, he wanted more of that kind of action and took up one of Charlie's spare fly rods. He started catching pinks as fast as I, stripping pink marabou streamers through the hole.

The next day brought more of the same. The wind was down from 30 to 20 knots, mixed with a number of rain showers. Cool weather in the low 40's time for winter steelheading sportswear. Another morning spent drifting for trout and the afternoon casting to salmon. In one sequence we rounded a bend in the river to see a large Brown bear just about to cross from one braid to another. We rolled in close with the jet sled to snap a few pictures, however Mr. Brown bear was not in a photogenic mood, and slipped easily into the bush headed for the back side of the island. We raced around to catch him coming out the other side, but again he escaped the cameras and doubled back. Time to give up the chase and open up the lunch box. Just as we did , the wind and rain picked up considerably and so we raced back to the le-ward side of the island to escape the elements. The same side the bear was last seen traveling towards. Sitting tucked up alongside the island with the bushes just over my head...chewing on a fresh halibut salad sandwich I spent most of lunch looking over my shoulder to make sure Mr. Bear wasn't joining us for lunch. With so many salmon in the river, the bears were way more interested in fish then human flesh, yet you can never be too careful with a 1000 pound Brown bear.

In the evenings around 8 PM a couple of us would run up the river and fish for pinks and silvers. Jody our guide would drop us off at a productive hole and leave us for a couple hours. In late August you still have enough light to fish until 10 PM. One evening I went to our little honey hole by myself and as I leaped off the bow of the boat onto the tundra I intruded on a 700 pound brown bear 15 yards away standing there looking at me with a huge salmon clamped in his teeth. Like a dog protecting a fresh prime rib bone, this big fella spun on his heels and bounded away at top speed, the salmon flopping up and down out both sides of his mouth. Only in Alaska. *(More on that Later in the Playing with Bears essay)*

Since most of the pinks were in the three to six pound range, I opted to try and catch some with my 5 weight nine foot Loomis. I decided to drift an egg pattern higher in the water column and on the second cast the rod was almost ripped from my grasp as a fresh silver in the 15 pound range inhaled my size 10 fly. I got about four gray-hound leaps out of the big male before we parted ways. I landed eight or nine nice pinks, when I hooked up with another silver. This one topped out at 12 pounds and was landed within a couple minutes. I caught two more smaller silvers before I heard Jody fire up the jet boat to come retrieve me.. While the fishing action was hot I, kept checking my six for large brown furred fishermen.

In Alaska, dogs are one of the most valuable partners an outfitter has. Not just sled dogs, but bear dogs. We had the pleasure of having Grizzly a chiseled yellow lab watching over our humble camp. Griz earned that name for two reasons. First he was guarding the camp for bears, and second this dog loved to fish just like a bear. If you had a rod and were casting around camp, Griz was right on your heels. Play a fish and Griz was there to net it for you in his teeth. We had just turned in, when Griz started to bark. This was a very excited bark. Much more excited than normal. (Griz barked at salmon all day long). Turns out a large bear was trying to step out of the water and come into camp. Griz was in the water with the bear trying to discourage his visit. The bear did not appreciate the dog's hospitality and growled at the dog while snapping his teeth. Griz was relentless, so Jody realizing that the bear might enjoy the dog for a midnight snack, ran to his tent, grabbed his shotgun, and lobbed a few rounds over the bear's head to make him understand once and for all, he was not welcome. The gun fire got his attention, and off he went.

On Thursday afternoon I had the pleasure of fishing with Trapper. Up to this point Trap had been guiding Woody and his daughter Connie. I was interested in fishing with Trapper because he was a home town guy. Trapper runs his own guide business and lodge on the banks of New York's famous Salmon River from Sept. until May when he returns to Alaska. I was at home in Alaska with the style of fishing we were doing. Egg pattern fishing is the heartbeat of catching trout and salmon in the Lake Ontario tributaries back in western NY.

The day had turned out bright and sunny. Temperature was probably in the mid 60's. We spent a few minutes sighting a number of pools as we meandered up river. Finally settling on a turn that created rips and seams along the edge of a deep calm bay. The silvers swung in and out of the edge of this seam to feed on roe. I had to wade in above my waist to present the fly in a stealthy manner to not spook the fish. Casting up stream and out over the rip, the current swung my bug in along the seam. With just a tiny pinch of split shot to keep the fly from raising too fast on the swing the first silver smashed my fly on the third cast. The trick was to hook a fish from the pod...then back pedal out of the run and get the fish in the calm water bay so we wouldn't break up the convention of silvers lazily hanging on the seam. This first fish had "Other " ideas however. He refused to be played in the bay, and bounded up river heading for the bend. No way to catch up to him. I got him turned the first time, but on his second sprint out of the run he pulled free. As I repositioned myself for the next assault, I was able to find the sweet spot in which to steer the fish into the right fighting water. The next five fish put up valiant fights, but we managed to slip a net under them. They ranged in size from a few pounds to double digits, some with big kypes on their jaws and red sides, while others were as silver as a newly minted dime.

The afternoon was getting long, and I could almost taste the steaks on the menu for dinner that night. Trap and I picked up and headed down river scouting some other holes for Silvers. As we wheeled around a hair pin turn, we caught a huge brown bear swimming in the water. Trap swung the jet rig hard to port and I dug in my vest for my camera....caught the big bear just as he reached shore, not 30 feet away. Close ups of bears is the rich butter cream frosting on the cake in this wild paradise.

My last evening in camp we had another feast fit for kings. After supper under cloudless skies, we opted to hit the pink and silver hole one more time a quarter mile up from camp. Jody dropped Woody, Rob and I off one last time. Just like clockwork I saw off in the distance my friend the brown bear. He appeared to be the same animal I'd run into the other night. For once the fishing was more difficult. The fish had lock jaw, and we had to get creative with some of our fly selections. Woody, showed me a fly he bought from a catalog before the trip. This thing was NOT very pretty. He offered me a few...and I politely declined. Well you can just about guess what happens next. Woody, ties on this nasty looking critter, whips it out in the direction of some migrating silvers. Immediately his rod tip bows low to the water as a thick shouldered Coho inhales the fly and dashes off downstream with Woody whooping and hollering over his shoulder something about the price of one of these hot flies should Rob or I be interested. Woody lands this bright silver buck, then catches a nice pink salmon on the same ugly fly. I told him one more fish, and I'm buying. Luckily for me I hung a couple pinks and a silver on my standard feathers before Jody picked us up for the last time.

Needless to say Woody had quite a monologue about the fly and the fish as we sat around camp on our final night together. Now I wished I had grabbed one of those silver catching beauties for a keep sake.

Sat. Morning and around noon I was changing out back to King Salmon. Because of the packing I had to do...I opted to pass on a two hour fishing jaunt to get one last long drink of this magical place. After Breakfast, while Trapper took Woody, Connie and Rob fishing....I decided to take a hike back behind camp with Griz. I didn't have a weapon, but with the dog I felt safe in not spooking a bear. We climbed to the top of a hill that over looked the whole river valley. What a sight. I saw something moving down at the bend of the river where we had fished almost every night. I put the binoculars on the object. Probably the same bear we'd been jumping every night, fishing the hole. It was a fitting end to a trip filled with dreams.

Taking off from a river that is bleeding along at about seven or eight knots in a single engine Cessna is one experience that is a big part of what Alaska is all about. The bush pilots are the ultimate taxi service. As Scooter drifted off the small island where we kept the jet boats backwards down the river.....he craned his neck from side to side, trying to keep her centered up in the deeper part of the flow. Seems like we drifted down stream for 10 minutes. Scooter needed a lot of run way to get the sleek white bird off the water. Plus our runway had a curve to the left and some shallow gravel bars we had to avoid. Over the roar of the engine I heard him ask my guide Jody who was hitching a ride back to King Salmon for a recap of where the deepest water was located on our take off path. That gets your attention that while the guys who fly the wilderness of Alaska make it look easy.... they have to be on top of their game on every trip.

Scooter found the sweet spot in the flow and off we went...one last look at the Alaska Trophy Adventures out camp as we screamed by and up we went just clearing a stand of jack pines as we banked to starboard. Another 30 minute flight over the Tundra to King Salmon. Same silly smile on my face as when I arrived and caught that first fish. You can read about this place...see fishing shows and documentaries about wild Alaska, but until you have ventured into the wilderness and experienced it firsthand you'll never truly understand what makes this place so special for the many who live or visit there. I never met a single angler or hunter on this trip who were in Alaska for the first time. All were returning for the third or fourth trip. There was no doubt I'd be back.

5

Salty Silvers
(Prince William Sound Alaska)

THE STURDY DE-HAVILLAND Otter engine roaring wiggled to the left and banked around a stand of jack pines on the edge of a rock mound that looked a little too close as we brushed on by. The beach was just below us, and at 100 feet the waves breaking on shore looked "Energetic". White foam licked the shoreline over and over, and I wondered if we might have picked the wrong day to take two handed fly rods to Prince William Sound in hopes of hooking bright silvers cruising the salty shoreline.

My thoughts? if those breakers look that high way up here, I could just imagine what they must be like at sea level. White water rushing the beach like the 85 Bears defense on third and long. The Otter came to a stop about 20 yards from shore and we started to pile out. Rods, packs, lunches were handed down. Our guide said just get into shore and you'll find a path to the beach. We had to cut through a little meadow and a couple small stands of stunted pines to get to the volcanic rock and kelp-laden beach.

I'll digress for just a moment. On the way to the beach we came around a stand of alders, and there in the clearing was an old Military tent. Sitting in camp chairs smoking (I'm sure pure Cuban cigars, cause they can get them in Russia) was a group of anglers from Mother Russia, drinking Vodka singing and raising hell. They greeted us with hearty bellowing hello's as we traipsed on by. They were camping and fishing the salt and I doubt they had checked in through customs and for sure I didn't want to ask. The things you run across in Alaska!

We came up over a knoll and there it was, Little Johnstone Bay on Prince William Sound. Like little kids scrambling for the beach back home with sand pal and shovel dangling from our arms, we rushed to a little gradient up on the beach where our spare gear would stay dry.

Fish were breaking everywhere and some were air born, but they didn't look very bright. The fish were seeking this little stream we had followed to the sea. The tide was low, and the gravel bar was piled high enough to form a barrier so the tributary couldn't reach the salt. Yet the fish still hung around waiting for the doors to open. Turns out these fish were pink salmon. My first experience with Pink salmon in Alaska several years before was they'd hit any stripped fly. Not so this time, these fish were not interested. I stepped into the surf, the rollers were timing out at about four seconds per wave, hardly a lot of time to make traditional Spey cast. I had to get the line out as far as I could and strip like mad before the next wave grabbed your fly and fly line and tossed it at your feet. I managed to make a few good casts, got the timing down and stripped the fly through some good looking water. But that surf was heavy, and it was knocking me around pretty good. It looked impossible to move out past the surf line as the bottom dropped out of sight quickly.

Maybe I thought it was a mirage as I scrolled down the beach about a quarter mile, it appeared the surf was calmer. I noticed another angler fast to a good fish and this fish appeared to be salmon-esc, as it jumped and ran out the line on his spinning rod. "Hmmmm", looks calmer. Maybe a pod of Silvers in that area. It was time to investigate. I grabbed my pack and headed down the beach. The sand was black in places from the volcanic fall out and the sand would disappear beneath my feet if I walked in the surf.

I neared the angler who had the fish on, walked another 100 yards past that group, and found a little calm water, with little or no kelp washing up on the beach. I tied on a green and white concoction we had spun up the night before, fired a decent 90-foot cast past the froth that still hissed at my feet, and started the quick strip. I repeated the process twice more and on the fourth cast my line stopped as if I had stuck the fly in the side of a building. The water beyond the crest of the next wave blew up and a heafty silver salmon exploded into the air.

In an instant, the big reel started to hum as the excited fish headed out to sea. I quickly rolled the rod to the same side, and applied steady side pressure. 14 foot of Spey rod curved around in a tight "C' turning the fish back to shore. Then another blistering run, I worked the rod from one side to the other pulling line back across the fishes head making him turn and tire out. In a few moments after a couple more knuckle busting runs I eased him up on the beach. I sat in the surf admiring this solid Coho salmon laying at my feet, covered in sea lice, it's muscles still bulging from our encounter. I snuck him back into the surf and the roar of the ocean seemed to increase as if to say thank you for giving this treasure back to the salt.

Turn the clock back twenty four hours earlier, the four of us, Dave, Todd, Gratson and myself had talked to our guide Mark Glassmaker about coming up with a little more challenging day on the water. To that point we had done the 100 fish day gig in hitting some spots that were gimmie's. Not that we didn't appreciate all the action, and the fish hard fighters, leaping and running all over the

"Fish On"

place, but it was like fishing in a backyard pond stocked to the brim with salmon and trout.

We needed a little more challenge so Mark said he'd stop by our cabin that night and give us a couple other options for fly outs. We were cooking out on the grill when Mark pulled up in his truck to lay out some other choices. He got to Prince William Sound last. It's funny when somebody hits the right note in this kind of conversation, and everybody lights up at the same time to the suggestion. Fresh silver in the salt, sea lice, open water. It was a done deal, Prince William Sound it is.

Mark left, and we munched on Italian sausage and fresh silvers from the day before. Washed them down with a few swigs of Alaskan Kodiak Brown a delicious Alaskan microbrew. "Let's see, salt-water fishing how we fixed for flies" I asked? We looked at each other and for a moment our hearts sank. All we had with us were the traditional pink, purple and cerise colors that Alaskan river silvers, dollies, and rainbows crave. These files might not be the ticket for salt-water fly-fishing. I started to dig through my portable fly tying pack. I found some stick on eyes, some white materials, a little black, some greens, barbell eyes but no other materials that are normally used in tying salt water bugs.

The bigger problem? There were no real fly shops around. The shops we stopped at so far carried the same style of flies we had al-ready tied. Hell, Dave and Todd had tied about five or six boxes of flies, and nothing that resembled the standard salt-water patterns. We took a walk over to Marks house from our cabin and asked if he had any materials or knew what colors the silvers were hitting in Little Johnstone Bay. Of course he listed every color we didn't have. The Greens, Whites and Blues that would be last on our list of materials for the general Kenai River and surrounding tributaries.

Still Dave and Todd set out to see what they could find in town, while Gratson and I got started with what I had. With one vice, we took turns tying up flies, epoxy some eyes on the heads and we gener-ally put together a couple dozen suitable salt-water flies. We were up till about midnight with a 4:30 AM wake up call to get to the Charter plane base. But sleep didn't come easy with the thoughts of fresh silver salmon dancing in our dreams.

My very first Alaskan salt water fish on the fly, and it was everything I could have hoped for. This was no picnic and our guide met our requirements to put us in an area with plenty of fish but we had to work hard for them. Make good casts find the right stripping speed, sink rate, and fly profile. It took some playing around and with several adjustments to find the sweet spot. Unless you are my friend Gratson. Gratson the only one of the four of us with a single hand rod had a light green and white barbell eyed Clouser style fly. On about his second cast, he hooks a beautiful silver that runs him deep into his backing. He lands the fish only to discover, the fish chomped down on the head of the fly and broke one of the lead eyes off. Undaunted, Grat rose from the surf and two casts later was tight to another big Coho as it steamed away with his one eyed fly.

My fifth fish landed that day; turned out to be close to 15 pounds, and simply steam rolled my fly on about the second strip after the drop. This fish just about jerked the rod out of my hand burring the tip into the swollen surf then switched gears and headed for mother Russia. This last fish made seven runs for freedom, until Mark's slid him up into the wash. The green and white fly turned out to be the overall fly of choice, except for Gratson's one eyed wonder in a lighter green. I did play with some of my river patterns and they did end up working. The cerise, and an aqua colored Spey pattern took a couple nice fish, and turned a few more.

The guides marveled at the tool we used that day to get into fish on the fly. They weren't used to having anglers firing two-handed rods in the surf, with guys who could make 100-foot casts and cover a lot of water. This allowed us to get into about 25 nice fish between the four of us. But the key was being able to switch cast or even overhead cast these big sticks. The power of the two hander also was a bonus in locking down on a rampaging fish.

The water in Little Johnstone Bay drops off quickly from the beach.

This ledge just off the beach created the structure for the fish to cruise the shoreline, and still feel safe with the proximity to deeper water. Weighted flies, as well as sink tips were the order of the day. A full sinking line would have been difficult to handle in the rushing surf with the quick frequency of the waves. So we employed LC13 and T14 materials in building our own tips. I build them in different lengths and played with the different lengths until I found the one that got me into the strike zone. On this day, tips in the 10 to 12 foot range got us into biting fish. But I carry an assortment from 3 feet to 15 foot to work on my adjustments in finding the right sink tip length for the fishing situation.

The most difficult task when trying to strip fish with a 14 foot rod is to keep rod balance as you strip. We didn't have stripping baskets and I'm not sure because of the casting movement with a two handed rod a stripping basket would be easy to use. If the ocean was calm with little or no wash on the beach, one could load the rod in traditional two handed fashion for Spey style casting and make good long presentations. But we found with the wave frequency, we either had to make overhead casts which can be a little uncomfortable when moving a 14 foot stick back over your casting shoulder.

Or we had to switch cast, a method almost like a roll cast to pick up a line, anchor it by moving the rod up and then to a 45 degree angle off your casting side and fire back out. The other key was to get the heavy sink tips to the surface before you made your switch or over hand cast.

The concentration to make a good cast while dealing with the surf is sometimes a deterrent to the attention one needs to pay in Alaska to their surroundings. You have to make sure you lift your eyes from the water line and gaze around the area. Fiords, and rock ledges surround little Johnstone Bay. Eyes out to sea you'll start to notice the flocks of sea ducks, and the swirl of sea lions, as they are also fishing for silvers. Along the mountain ridges you can make out sheep and goats grazing the edges of no man's land. This is a wild place, and you have to make sure you drink it all in.

Our guide challenged us with this adventure. We had to tie up special flies, we had to make good casts, and we had to work hard to get the speed of the fly down on the strip to have a silver make the commitment. In the end, exhausted, and wet from the pounding surf, muscles aching from long casts, and hard fighting fish, there was and air of accomplishment like winning the big game and this moment felt like sitting back in the locker room tired and beat up but happy for the victory.

The Otter flew overhead as it made its way into the little lake behind the beach. We packed up our gear, and trudged back to the plane. I noticed the ceiling dropping as the plane roared over our heads and in a few moments we met the pilot on the path as he was heading for the beach. There is nothing more comforting then "Grey haired" bush pilots in Alaska. However today our pilot had a worried look on his face. The weather was falling apart and we had to hurry out of there if we wanted to make it back on time, no less then leave and make it back at all. He told us to start loading the plane while he fetched the rest of his party.

This is the adventure that is remote fly ins in places like Alaska. You can't be too careful, relax too much in a place like this, because adversity and some danger is always looming. As we rocketed out of there just ahead of the nasty weather approaching from the west and looked out the window at the mountains and the glaciers we could finally sit back and claim victory. A day filled with hard fighting fresh silvers in the salt on last minute flies, and two handed rods. We had taken a shot at something different, something spur of the moment, Once again got to love it when a plan comes together.

Sea Lice Salty Silver

6

End of the World Steelhead

THIS BACK BRAID off the main stem of the river looked fishy, with the river high and flowing at about 6 knots, I figured the fish might find this migration route more plausible. I uncorked a cast slightly down stream, and guided the fly's path with the tip of my rod. As many as I've caught this way, I never get used to the jolt of a steelhead in its most primitive nature to SLAM the fly as it swings down near it's holding position. The jerking forward motion of my arm...and the rod tip that was parallel to the water was now bucking like a wild stallion trying to break out of his corral, and 10 pounds of silver muscle is air born ALL before my brain can process what is happening...it's a blur, BUT I get control of my faculties quickly enough to set the hook and lean the rod over all in one motion to stop the fish from rubbing me off on the submerged tundra tangle. The fish was relentless in trying to drag my line into the structure, but the 8 weight did its job and I was able to finally swing this chrome rocket to the gravel where head guide Patrick grabbed him and we snapped the traditional C&R hero shots.

Two hours into the trip and on the board – Bearing Sea Steel

Pat walked away and I roared a loud primal scream. A release of emotion that had built up inside my Steelheader's brain since 1998 some 13 years ago. Thirteen years of thinking about it, planning, then letting it go, then back to researching it once more. The Sandy River in the Aleutian Islands Chain of Alaska was allegedly the last frontier on the planet for pure bread ocean run Bering Sea Steelhead. And laying before me was 10 pounds of bright chrome and muscle covered in sea lice. The adrenalin rush from having sealed the deal in the first half hour of fishing in this remote river, was nothing short of exhausting. Two days to get here from Rochester NY....and as soon as I loosened my grip on his tail my prize sped back into the low 40 degree flow and as quickly as the success had come, the game was reset to start all over again.

Two hours before this first fish, Lifting off from Port Moller (Population 2 in October) and flying the 12 minutes to our camp on the Sandy River ....I could view the coast line of the Bering Sea as it traced the outline of the Tundra below us...marked with pot holes of standing water, some blue lines of running water, and a patchwork quilt of tundra that was as desolate as the surface of the moon.

Charlie Banked the Piper Cub to line up the runway and we landed on a squishy cinder deck....and taxied up to four small tents and one large cook and gathering tent on the edge of this man made landing zone. The tents were tucked up in the Alders to escape the stiff breeze coming off the Sea. On the way in viewing the Sandy River from the air, there was no other sign of life, except for a half dozen lumbering Brown bears getting their last taste of fin flesh before finding a winter hibernation den. No crowds of shoulder to shoulder fishermen as we are accustomed to when Steelhead fishing in the Great Lakes.

Dave, Todd, Mark and I all anxious to string our rods and get after these mystical fish had to be careful to take care of business first. You see we were "CAMPING" in the Aleutians on the Sandy River. No cushy lodge with Sauna's and hot tubs, Rather...Cabala's tents, cots, and sub-zero sleeping bags were the order of the day. The cook and gathering tent hosted a small four seat table, with some canvas chairs that would be our living room for a week. Boxes and coolers with food

Home Sweet Home

surrounded the table, and a three burner Coleman stove would serve as the Most Valuable device for this week to number one heat the water for coffee in the mornings after sleeping in high 20's to low 30 temps on the night time tundra.

Camping for the four of us was a huge stretch. None of us had been camping in dozens of years if hardly ever. So the notion of staying warm and dry for seven days in a place where the weather changes in seconds let alone minutes was a much bigger challenge for us then swinging streamers and catching these historic fish. We knew we had the skills to catch fish, what we were very unsure of, was our ability to handle the sometime brutal elements the Aleutians can deal you in October.

The Sandy River is located about a third of the way down the Aleutian chain, and it's jagged mountain range includes several active Volcanoes. Early in the week, we were shrouded in a low ceiling with intermittent rain and didn't have much of a view to these mountains. By Wednesday, the skies started to clear each day and while the weather remained in the low 40's and was usually accompanied by a stiff 15 to 25 knot breeze, we were rewarded with the full splendor of this desolate place. Jagged peaks, fully snow covered mountains, and flat tops with steam billowing out of them. Trace your site line to the river valley and you had the stark contrast of where the mountain range bottomed out into the river valley. In early Oct, the river valley is still somewhat green,

One measure of the success and effectiveness of an Outfitter and guide service is their ability to prepare their sports for what to expect in a fishing or hunting environment to include a complete list of what gear to bring, and maybe more important what gear NOT to bring. Charlie and Pat, provided a packing list to our team that after the trip was complete and we can reflect on how helpful it was...I'd have to say it was the most complete list of what we'd need to bring that I've ever received. We followed the list to a T. In doing so we stayed warm dry and safe throughout the seven days in camp. Save of course the "Get Your Attention" cold slap in the face we received climbing out of our sleeping bags in the middle of the night to take a leak, or in the morning to get up and get started.

Day Two, and the Loss of our most important Asset.

Sunday night Todd and I had scored our first steelhead of the trip, while Dave had landed a migrating silver and stuck the Iron into two steelhead that managed to escape a beaching. As we stepped into the Cook tent the delicious smell of a full blown Spaghetti and Sausage dinner made this crazy wild place seem tame for the moment. We're hungry ...tired from all the travel, yet elated that we've found some fish in our Camp water....and it was only the first ½ day of the trip. Charlie announces Day 2 possibilities. Pat, Charlie and Apprentice guide in training Adam had set up camp three days before and had spent as much time as possible scouting fishing routes up and down river of our camp. Our temporary home was less than half way up the Sandy Rivers 18 mile run from a Tundra lake to the Bering Sea. Charlie said he'd like to take one guy, fly down to the beach at the mouth of the river with a high tide in the morning to see if they could catch a rush of fish streaming into the river. Dave volunteered to go. Todd, Mark and I would start at the camp water, and fish our way down river in small Water Master boats, where Pat and Adam had mapped out several take out points with hiking routes back to the camp. The longest stretch would take us below camp for about an hour hike back.

Day two dawns with drizzle, and light winds. A hearty helping of breakfast Taco's and coffee and we split up forces to see if we could pin down a mass migration of fresh Steel. Our team started at the camp water, and a ½ hour in, making a long cast to a gravel ledge that dropped into a trench my fly didn't travel 10 feet and my Beulah two hander starts doing the chrome dance and a double digit fish lights up the surface and skips across the water, then digs into the fast current and uses his mass to make the drag sing on my reel. This fish played tug of war for another couple minutes or so, and I finally led him into some gravel between two short tundra alders. I marveled at how perfect this fishes fins were. They were almost see-through, not curled or off color like a hatchery fish. Sea Lice clung to the fishes skin near his anal fin, and as was fish number one....was bright silver but this big buck had a hint of a scarlet stripe running the gauntlet of his center line.

Pat and I released the fish....so less then an hour of fishing and I had scored two bright lice covered fish. We worked our way down stream....and you could cut the anticipation with a knife at each run, riffle and pool, yet the fish weren't cooperating at all. At the $Million Dollar hole I had a good grab and set the hook, but knew right away this wasn't a big fish. Turned out to be a 15 inch rainbow that took an intruder almost half his size. We fished down through some Braids to the main stem, and still couldn't dig out a player.

A full day had slowly crept by as we neared the 50 minute take out. A bit weary from battling rain, and wind, we got to shore, buttoned up the Water Crafts, and started the hike along an ATV trail back to camp. Myself, I turned my thoughts to Dave and Charlie...maybe they had discovered the Mother Load of Steel down in the Estuary. Was anxious to get back to camp and see how they did which initiated a quicker pace to get some news. Along the route I flushed one covey after another of ptarmigan, and secretly wished I had packed my grouse gun. The walk back would have been a lot more exciting if we could hunt a few of these beautiful birds along the way.

The ATV trail led almost back to the Runway, but we had to cut through a few Alders to find the gravel lane....once we did, there was No Plane. Hum???? Man the fishing must have been off the hook, they aren't back yet and it's dinner time for sure, but heck if I was into fish, I wouldn't want to be on a timer either....except for getting back before dark. As we chatted our way into camp, the Cook Tent flap opened up and both Dave and Charlie stepped out with a look in their eyes that didn't signal good news.....and it wasn't.

They had landed on the beach and fished the estuary hard until about 2 PM. No love from any fish down there, so Charlie decided to run up river with the Piper, and get Dave into some main stem water about 12 miles up from the Salt. Knowing we had gone down river hence getting a good look at a lot of water on the first full day to hope-fully zoom in on larger pods of fish. Upon approach to the Tundra runway up near an Alaska Fish and Game Outpost....the plane took a hop on first contact and when it landed again the force tore off the port landing gear slid the plane sideways spinning the prop into the tundra and sticking a wing tip into the ground.

Luckily neither Dave or Charlie were injured, but they were for sure stranded. Charlie assessed the damage and then his 25 years of guid-ing in the wilds of Alaska took over and he made finding a safe place to hold up his number one priority. There was an old Sauna there...but too small to hang out in. They opted to try and get into the Fish and Game camp, and Dave slipped through a window with Charlie follow-ing, and they would be safe, with food heat and provisions to stay dry and warm.

Their luck began to change when another outfitter guiding a Bear hunting party rode in on some ATV's and called in another Bush pilot to help them out. That's how Charlie and Dave got back to camp. So as Charlie began dinner on Monday night, we had a lot of balls in the air on what to do next. Charlie had another pilot coming in on Tuesday to take him back to King Salmon and get parts for the plane. The rest of us would be relegated to camp, without any motorized transport, and now had to figure out how to continue fishing. Mark, Todd and I hadn't much to report from Camp water down river. Our first inclination was to NOT go back and fish that water again right away. That meant only one option. Go up river with the one man water crafts, use them as two man crafts (3 boats...six guys)....and fish our way back to camp.

The Daily Death March

The daily trek in a vast land

Hiking on the Tundra with 30 to 35 pound packs in our waders and wading boots carrying our rods and fishing gear. OK....sounds do-able. Tuesday morning after breakfast we strapped on the gear and headed off for new water. Patrick had to assess how much pain we could handle in hiking the Tundra with our gear, and for sure having 20 year old Adam along didn't hurt as the kid was in fantastic shape and could huff one of the boats on his back. Our first days route took us out of camp and over the Tundra for about a mile, and then we'd cut back down to the river's edge and try to migrate up the shore line. We had to jump back up in the Alders a few times when the edge got a little thin.

We ended between two to three miles upriver, and the hike took us about two hours. Slogging on the Tundra is like walking on a mat-tress, couple with the fact that the Tundra is a puzzle of moguls one has to plan each step carefully so as not to turn an ankle or knee. We arrived at a run that dropped into a pool and tail out to gravel that set us up with enough room to push four anglers through with several fish holding areas. We found out later this was known as Rocket Run.

We spread out and began rotating through the run, about five minutes in I get the hard tug at the apex of my swing, and have a fish cart wheeling down river. I wanted to get below him, but didn't think I could cross a trench between me and shore.....laid the rod over to stop his run, and pulled the hook....just as I was booting that fish, Dave lit up a real nice chrome rocket in my back pocket, two fish in less than five minutes appeared to be a good sign of things to come. Dave landed his fish, and we reset the rotation.

No more Hookups in the Rocket so into the boats and down to the next likely spot. We pulled over on a gravel bar with a classic shift in the river from right to left dropping out of some fast water and gravel through a nice deep run with a seam down the middle separating the roily water and a nice migration trench for the fish to matriculate up river.

Todd positioned himself at what would become the number two slot we'd fish all week. Plenty of fish were pinned at "Mink Run" (Named for an ornery Mink who wasn't spooked that 6 guys were trampling around his island) right where the fast water dumped and mixed in at the slot between the heat and slack water.

Only a couple casts in and Todd was tight to a really nice double digit fish....after a few jumps and runs Patrick tailed this metal maniac and snapped some pictures. With Dave Todd and I already having some action, we had Mark take the next rotation, and Mark wasn't into his fifth cast and step when his rod lit up with another sea lice covered track star. At this point the entire team had successfully beached a steelhead which was our number one goal.

We caught some resident rainbows and Dolly Varden in this slot and then continued to move down towards camp. On this day we hit at least two steelhead in each spot, which became the model until Patrick and Todd found "Break-a-two-e Run".

The Karma Kid Makes A Huge Comeback

My buddy Dave and I are aligned on good Karma. In three trips to the Great State for he, Todd and I, we always started the trip on the first evening at the "Blue Fox" in Anchorage. A nothing in particular bar/restaurant in a strip mall that serves decent steaks, and good Alaskan micro-brews. It's tended by a gal named Mandy who has the same thirst for fishing Alaska as we do. We rumble in, sit down order a drink and dinner and get all the area updates North and South of Anchorage on where the hot fishing is, and Mandy's reports are usually accompanied by a cell phone photo or two. As we arrived on Oct 1, with an overnight at our other must stay favorite "The Alaska House of Jade"….we stowed our gear and headed out for dinner. I thought our only destination could possibly be the Blue Fox. However Todd's target food was a real steak joint. There are a few chain places in Anchorage that are good, and we didn't know of any local specialty steak house, so we wandered up the road towards Chain food alley. All the while I was dropping the karma case…and Dave was picking up on it. Between Dave and I we finally talked Todd and Mark into the Fox…and even though we were literally IN the Cattleman's restaurant parking lot, we doubled back to the Fox.

Sure enough Mandy was in true form, didn't necessarily remember us from our last 2008 trip, but none the less we talked fishing, she shared pictures, we ended up getting a very good steak dinner, and enjoyed the local Micro brews. And Dave and I had successfully aligned the stars ALMOST.

Fast forward to first night in camp and Dave volunteers to take the somewhat fateful plane ride on Monday with Charlie. So two days into the trip , while Dave has hooked a couple chromers, he hasn't beached one, and he's been into a "rough landing". Tuesday as he hooked and landed his first Sandy steelhead, the skies were about to open up for him. He would be repaid in spades for his misfortunes of Sunday and Monday, and from Tuesday on, Dave was as hot as one can get fishing to migrating fish where you have to rake them out of hiding here and there.

But Dave isn't lucky, he's just very good, and didn't matter if he was the first caster down a run, or the fourth, he was a fish magnet and put some really beautiful fish to the beach. Dave dug fish out of some very tight holding water that opened up our eyes for the rest of the week, that while there were plenty of tailor made runs and pools, the fish were in pocket water as well, and we learned not to pass by any likely looking spots.

Dave finding the sweet spot on Muskrat Run

On Thursday, head guide Pat once again moved our float boats across a particular crossing spot ... up an embankment back down the other side and across as part of our trail of tears routine up river each day. Pat had noticed this nice boulder strewn slot as he was climbing up off the stream bank each day. So he and Todd stopped in there, and banged some fish right away.

Next day, Todd, Dave, and Mark hooked into 8 steelhead in this slot, and in doing so landed some nice chrome and broke a couple rods. So this spot earned the nickname Break-A-Two-E run. From the river bank on the opposite side, this run didn't look like much at all. This was just an example of water the Upper lodge jet sleds sped by everyday with their sports to fish the gravy water up and down the river. We fished it the last day, I hooked a nice big rainbow, Dave and Pat each landed a steelhead, and we had a couple other plucks from fish. The three day total in this 100 foot run was at least 20 pulls on the swing.

Each day ended at the Camp water ...that was truly good to all four of us. We all had numerous hook ups in the main stem and back braid of our jumping out point. The main stem tumbled out of a fast curvy run into a slot that was gravel lining the bank and a ledge that dropped into a migration lane. On the casting bank....a trench five feet off shore ran the length of this gravel Bar. We hooked fish dropping flies off the ledge or on the hang down in the trench. Most of the fish hooked over the week came in either of these two scenarios , very few mid river shots or across gravel bars.

The Karma Kid

The last night Charlie and Pat the rescue pilot flew back into camp with Charlies Piper Cub finally repaired and checked out back in King Salmon. It was October in the town of King Salmon. The General store about to close for the season had a 12 pack of beer and one bottle of Jack Danial's left on the bare shelves and the boys brought them in for a last night campfire and celebration. We built a campfire with what little dry wood and sticks we could find and finished all the beer and bourbon. The night fell silent, windless, no rain or snow, and a billion stars in the sky from our Bering Sea vantage point.

The temperature had dropped well below freezing that night. Up once to pee, and could barely get the job done outside the tent on the frozen tundra. Next morning as we made coffee, we noticed the wings on both planes were iced up. Of course with no deicer available way out here in the middle of nowhere, we tried using different tools and stuff laying around camp to scrape the ice off. After awhile Pat the pilot had seen enough and told me to get all our gear and myself in his Super Cub, and he'd fly us back to Port Moller. Charlie would bring Dave, Todd, and Mark.

Now back in my early 20's I had actually done some flying, and while never soloing, had taken off and landed small planes. There was barely a breath of wind, and maybe because it was so subtle, Pilot Pat didn't fret about turning the plane to jump up in the wind, but rather pointed the Super Cub down the runway, and with the ever so slight tail wind gunned the engine. Off we went down this cinder lane heading for the Alders at the end, with me actually pulling back on an imaginary yoke to get her up, still Pat was waiting, and when he finally pulled back on the real yoke, we skipped up back down, and crashed straight onto the Alders, scrub and tundra flying everywhere. Somehow I never get tense in Bush planes even when things aren't going exactly as planned, and I was alert enough to think, Pat has a nose wheel plane. Not sure how he is going to pivot it back towards the runway, as we are chopping a new trail, and if the plane stalls, it will sink into the tundra, and we'll be on the SAT phone calling the Coast Guard to get the biggest helicopter they have to cradle a tow truck beneath it, and fly it from many miles away along the Bering Sea coast so we can pull Pat's plane out of the SHIT.

As this was all crossing my mind, Pat the rescue pilot somehow got the plane back up on the runway, an now taking off, we jumped up off the deck and we're airborne. I asked Pat how long he'd been flying bush planes in Alaska. He said over 30 years. I thought he must have started when he was 10. I also noticed our air speed was about 110 knots, when normally we should be at least 160? He said yeah we must have screwed something up on the plane... a Moment of silence and over the ear splitting roar of the engine, Pat looked at me and yelled "Cheated Death again Man….we cheated death again".

When we landed at Port Moller, we scrambled out of the plane to see what damage we had suffered. The tail flap had several tears in it. Before I could say anything Pat, ran to the cockpit, came back with a roll of duct tape, taped the flap back together, and then took back off to help Charlie with the others. Alaskan Bush pilots…..a very rare breed of men and women.

This trip was in my thoughts for over 10 years. Never seriously thought I'd ever get there. But we did it. Four guys who would never be considered hard core adventurers anymore (we were many years ago), kind of validated that while we typically wouldn't choose to rough it quite this much, if we had our eye on a target, and it meant camping hiking and fishing in one of the harshest places in the world, well we could pull it off. Was kind of a testosterone rush for me silly as it may seem. Dave, Todd, Mark and I all earned our platinum "Man Cards" on this adventure.

These Bering Sea fish were worth every minute it took….to get there!

7

Playing Nicely With Bears

I WOULD IMAGINE just about every angler who travels to fish Alaska has Alaskan Brown bear sightings on his or her checklist. I'd even venture to say that while they would enjoy seeing any bears, meaning black bears, the Alaskan Brown Bear is way more unique and in post trip conversation the mention of Black bears is more often an after thought, then part of the most interesting details of the stories told.

At the same time that most of us want to view some bears, none of us, (at least the sane individuals) want to be too close to these animals where there is any chance of an altercation. Now close to is all relative. Many times fishing rivers you'll have bears up or down river of you. They know we are there, we are a nuisance to them....we have to be. Bears know the best fishing spots, no different to a bear then to us when we find another angler occupying a favorite section of river. For the bears it's more a matter of life and death. They need to eat to survive the next cold Alaskan winter, we are just entertaining ourselves. So I have to believe bears get pissed off at seeing us in a spot they intended to fish. Most times they'll figure something else out, and won't try to force the issue. But it's "Never"...a "NEVER" with bears. They are unpredictable.

Worse yet is when either the anglers, or the bears figuratively and literally run into each other. Those situations are the deadliest of all.

While anglers are (or should be) acutely aware of bears while traveling in the bush, the bears....ahhh not so much. Most humans aren't pointing a gun at them. While they aren't actually at the top of the food chain, they are in the #1-A slot in Alaska.

Many would argue that a nasty bull moose is the King of the tundra and will kick a brown bears ass. However if the bear is as angry as the moose...my money is on the bear. He's nimble, much quicker, and can get to the defenseless end of the Moose to inflict mortal wounds with both teeth and claws. A Moose needs room to swing the ivory...A bear can fight in close dense quarters

So bears who trust their noses much more than their eye sight probably avoid many more confrontations with humans then one could imagine, if the wind isn't right and they can't smell us long before we meet, we end up in each other's laps...and hopefully it all goes well. The majority of anglers who travel to Alaska to fish do in fact check the bear sighting off their list. They will be in the presence of bears especially if they visit during or after the five salmon species runs. Yet the vast majority of these encounters end without incident, and I don't mean that to say the bear actually tried to attack or false charge them, but that they didn't have to yell at a bear, or move their position to accommodate the bears wishes.

Then there would be me. I and my friends and wife have had several closer than one would like encounters with large earth moving brown furry mammals. In 1998 on my first trip to the Great State....I mentioned earlier in the "My First Time (in Alaska)" portion of this memoir surprising a bear. Bristol Bay bears were some of the largest bears I've ever seen. There were a few that had to reach 1000 pounds or better. The only small bears I saw that week were cubs. Every adult bear was easily over 600 pounds.

When I went fishing on the evening in question by myself, many thoughts come to mind, that I would have a different answer for today. I would have questioned is it wise to go off by myself with only a fly rod in my hand. No gun or bear spray. I knew that I couldn't get back to camp if I was chased off by a bear, because there was a deep channel I'd have to cross to get back which would require me to shed my waders and swim across. I had no walkie-talkie...and cell phones were out of the question in the middle of nowhere. I'm not trying to get a readers reaction either that maybe the guide service should have been more careful. Maybe the kid from Montana should have stayed with me. I think the only reason he didn't is that I had displayed a confidence in my ability to handle the elements, the terrain, and was aware of my surroundings. I had been very careful. They hadn't seen a bear in this spot nor had we all that week. So we all got a bit careless, and lo and behold I stepped on a large 9 to 10 foot Brown bear.

It's purely amazing, and lucky that the bear didn't realize what a huge advantage he had over me at that moment. I'm 5' 11'....he's pushing twice my height and had me by 600 pounds. While I know he can't differentiate between a fly rod and a weapon, he knew to best protect his treasure of a 40 pound king salmon, he was best served by running away.

I can remember that moment as if it was frozen in time like a U-Tube video, and I can watch it over and over again in my mind, and I can still feel the emotion I had at the moment and how I reacted. I immediately went on the offensive. Stood my ground and screamed at him to get the fuck outta here. Yet this was the very first time I had ever been confronted by this type of situation. When he ran away....at that instant I remember thinking "Great...now I can fish". I was so di-aled into the huge pod of fish I had in front of me, and that I had them all to myself, a situation so rare in my home waters that one would never consider experiencing it. I wasn't nervous, it happened so fast I didn't have time to be scared. No second thoughts, not stopping for even an instant to say...heck I should wander away from this hot hole... that bear knows there are a lot of fish here as well...what's to stop him from regrouping and coming back for the Surf and Turf.

I jumped in the water and started catching fish...but I did now have a fresh sense of awareness, so I spent the remainder of the evening, two full hours before Jody returned looking over my shoulder, making sure he wasn't going to surprise me. I also made sure I stayed out in the water, far enough that bears could easily see me, and know I was there. I never gave it a second thought. I paced off the distance from my foot prints in the bank to where the bear had bear laying chewing on his salmon. It was less than 15 yards. I had also never experienced a bear standing up on his hind legs. I realize it's a defense mechanism to show a possible threat to the intruder.

I never hesitated to going back to that exact same spot the next night with Rob, and Woody. Once again we were dropped off. We didn't have an escape route had we encountered another bear or bears. We didn't have guns or bear spray, and they knew about my experience the night before, and none of us, or at least none of us expressed concern out load to each other. So I was lucky. I've read many bear attack stories since that day in 1998, and now realize more than ever I was dam lucky. The moral to this story is that it was Good that I wasn't scared at all....and it was very bad...that I wasn't scared at all.

Crescent River Encounters

Crescent River and Crescent River Lake is over on West Cook Inlet. It is a completely wild place at the base of a Volcano. There is one lone camp on the lake that never seems to be occupied. The only way in here is by float plane. In 2006 Lind's and I were in this part of the world. We had been having a ball fishing the road tribs on the Sterling and Seward highway. Lind's was new to fly fishing, but as mentioned before was the quickest leaner I've ever been around on how to handle the long rod. So she was on her own for the most part catching lots of Rainbows, Dolly Varden, and Sockeyes.

While Lind's had been to Alaska on a couple other occasions, and she'd been in bush planes, yet she hadn't run off to a remote place to spend the day. She and I waltzed into West Alaska Air service and asked where they were flying to catch Silvers. The manager said they had been running over to Crescent River and lake to hit some fish. We didn't really need a guide, just a ride. They had a group going over the next day, and the guide said he'd accommodate us by dropping us off with his raft in a decent spot and then take care of his sports. Come get us at the end of the day, and we'd all fly back to Kenai City. Sounded perfect

The next day we were actually fogged in for a couple hours but about 10 AM, we were loaded up in the Otter and on our way. This was only about a ½ hour flight. The guide pointed to the confluence where the lake dumped into the river. Said he'd drop us off there to start, go get his folks settled in, then come back and move us to a really good spot. The raft ride took a couple minutes and he headed back to get his party who was in need of more guiding then we were. Now while Lind's was easily handling the fishing on her own, she was still a tad unsure of getting everything rigged right and since we had to break our rods down for the flight in, I had to start from scratch. In a few minutes I had her ready to go, and she waded in and started fly fishing.

I had to start my rod from scratch as well...and I was distracted watching her, hoping that within the first few casts she's hook something anything. So I was taking much longer than normal. Lindsay turned back towards shore and stopped. "Dave there is a bear coming down the beach". We were on a point, I was around the far side of the point, and couldn't see back up the beach that Lind's had a view of. "Well how far away is he", "He's up where we landed, but he's walking this way". "Well he'll wind us pretty soon, and stop and go another direction. Go ahead and fish, we'll be careful". I get back to trying to get my gear together, and Lind's who now is more interested in the bear and his where a bouts then fishing says again "He's still coming"... "Don't worry about it honey"...we'll be all set. I have my head down... looking for my split shot in one of the packs, when I noticed Lindsay now out of the water is grabbing the other pack, my box of flies...."Hey what the hell are you doing Lind's, I'm still trying to get rigged up"... she says "I'm gathering up all our stuff for when we have to run from the bear", What do you mean run from the bear...where the hell is this bear"...she turns and pulls me around the corner..."THE BEAR IS RIGHT THERE". Holy shit...this bear has its head down, the wind is in our face meaning he can't wind us....he's trotting along without a care in the world. Now we have no place to go. The bramble and brush is way too thick to run into. The water is way too deep to wade across. I jump on a log ..start waving my arms like a crazy man, and screaming at the bear, "We are fishing here, get the FUCK OUTTA here (heck it worked

"Alaskan Brown"...not the beer, just its name sake

back in "98""). The Bear stops in its tracks and has this Oh shit look in its eyes, spins on a dime, and takes off like a freight train galloping up the beach.

I look up the beach and to my ultimate dismay I see six Frozen anglers standing in a huddle watching this beast come at them at a speed humans can't comprehend if they've never seen it before. Just then the guide comes around the corner, and he sees this play opening up before him, and guns his motor to race up there, at the same time screaming at these guys to throw something, wave their arms... anything. These guys are FROZEN...they either can't hear the guide because they are too far away, or they are so scared, they've lost their hearing. They never moved....and what happened next is a testament to how incredibly nimble these animals are. The bear ran right at them, there was a little pool in the corner of the beach in front of them, the bear jumped into the pool, not but a few feet where they were frozen, all in one motion, stuck his head underwater, came up with a struggling Silver Salmon, maintained procession of the fish while it tried to flop out of his mouth, made a 90 degree cut to his left and ran into the thickest brush imaginable as if it wasn't there.

It was over, took all of about 25 or 30 seconds, encompassed 8 or nine humans, and one now deceased and eaten salmon. I had never ever witnessed such wilderness craziness as I did that day. Now I was hoping I didn't mess up things with Lindsay. She either was thinking I was a brave hero, or an idiot for not listening to her. The way I figured it..."Hero"...since we wouldn't have any other moves where we were located other than to stand our ground.

Crescent River Lake Take II

In 2008, Lind's, Dave, Todd and I went back to Alaska on another Kenai Peninsula DIY'er trip. We picked up an air service near Soldotna that was running some silver trips. We wanted to get to an island off of Seward, that had a large run of BIG silvers, but the day we wanted to go it was very iffy with the weather. They said they could probably get us out there but couldn't guarantee getting's us back. Since we were day tripping we weren't prepared to camp overnight. We did have a guide lined up for this trip because this destination was a bit dicey and having a guide along was a smart move. We pondered our next move and they mentioned they could get us in and out of Crescent Lake and River. Lind's and I had been there and past the Bear situation, we had a great time and caught plenty of fish. So we said deal and off we went.

The water was very high in the lake and river, meaning there was little or no beach to walk. The guide had a skiff hidden in the brush, so he would take one or two of us up and down river to cast to Silvers, while the rest of us would wade close to shore and also try and hit some silvers. Ladies first and Lindsay got to run up river in the boat and sure enough landed a big silver. Meanwhile, Dave, Todd and I had also hit a few fish. The guide asked if we were keeping any fish, and we said no because the next day was our last, we had an all-day drift boat trip planned and wouldn't have time to have any fillets flash frozen to take back east.

So he asked, well do you mind if I take a few back. Of course not. So he strung the fish, and put them up on the shore of our base camp. Dave and Todd were next to run out on the skiff, while Lindsay and I hit the shoreline. This place is filthy with bears. And the problems is, with the high water the bears were up in the brush, so you didn't see them until they jumped a fish along the shore. Across the river from us...a big 800 pounder found a foothold and stepped out on a tiny patch of land. He was across the river. He spied us and wasn't the usual disinterested in us. In fact he jumped into the river about 50 yards from where Lindsay stood and started to swim at her. He had the wind in his favor so he knew we weren't fish or Moose...or....WAIT a minute..... the fish, we had five or six bright fresh silvers laying in the grass......we yelled to the guide who was just about the same distance as the bear, only up river. He saw what was happening, fired up the outboard. ... and roared in on the bear turning him back with the boat...and then came picked up the fish, and kept them in the boat the rest of the day. This little maneuver included "Washing" the fish smell out of the grassy bank where they were laying.

The last little tidbit from this story again is the fact that the bears couldn't be seen until they were on top of you. With the high water lapping the shore into the tree line...we wadded just a few feet from shore. Your back was 10 feet from the brush. When it was time to go we had spread out a bit in this little bay and continued to hook running jumping silvers stripping streamers. The guide came along to each of us and had us jump in the boat. Dave was fishing off a little point. We picked Dave up last, and as we rounded the point, and 800 pound bear was only 20 yards from where Dave stood...and he never knew the bear was moving up his way.

RUSSIAN RIVER SURPRISE

On the same 2008 trip, our base camp was a cabin in quaint Coppers Landing. We were minutes from the famed Russian River on the Kenai Peninsula. One of the DIY'er trips we had planned was to hike the four miles to the Russian River Falls, and then fish all the way back down to the confluence of the Russian and the Kenai river. The trail is very well marked and groomed. It is also major bear country. Lots of bears in this area of the Kenai Peninsula. In fact we stay at a wonderful B&B (The Alaska House of Jade) on each trip the day we arrive in Anchorage. Overnight and then head off on our adventure. While sitting in Dee's kitchen the morning we were leaving the B&B she recanted several stories of bear attacks in the Cooper Landing area. Even one right near her place in Anchorage. It appeared to be a high alert season in 2008 for bear encounters.

We were armed with Bear Pepper Spray courtesy of our Host Dee at the B&B who had purchased a couple canisters for us before we arrived. The trick hiking in Alaska bear country is to be loud and make noise. This way you hopefully avoid the surprise encounter which always seemed to be the most dangerous. We had a four mile hike up the mountain, and Lindsay led the singing for the full hike and while we saw some scat piles, none were steaming or fresh, and no fresh tracks.

We came upon the falls and the upper Russian that was truly a breath taking mountain stream. Dropped our packs traded hiking shoes for waders and wading boots and proceeded to enjoy a full day of catching beautiful leopard spotted rainbows and olive green and pink spotted Dolly Varden. While the day was overcast, it was mild, and the trip down river was totally uneventful, except for all of us catching and booting a few high class fish. We had parked the car in a lot nearest the trail up to the falls. We had planned to fish about a mile below that walk out, ...then hike back to the truck.

We finally waltzed up on the final pool of the day. I was overly satisfied with my luck that day. Some really fine fish to hand. We had all done well, so I decided to break down my rod and sit on this beautiful bank and watch my friends and Lind's fish.

I think I had reached into my day pack and located my Camera. While sitting out the last dance of the day, I started to peruse through the photo's we had snapped, selfishly interested in the three rainbows in the low to mid 20 inch range that I had managed to fool with a fly, and ultimately land. Every few seconds I looked up to survey Lindsay and my friends to see if they were connected to a fish. Todd had decided to go down below us a little further. He was now located down river and a large bush and underbrush was blocking my view of Todd. I could see his fly rod on each cast, but he was now out of my vision cone.

I remember looking up stream at Dave, pan down from him to in front of me watching Lindsay, and then below to where Todd's rod would make an appearance every time his line sizzled out to mid river. For Todd I was waiting to see his line taunt and hopefully a large rainbow or Dolly resisting his pulling on them by making a ruckus on the surface.

I had looked up from the camera and completed the panning of our crew maybe two or three times...when during the next time through this ritual, as I looked downstream, a huge brown furry head was sticking out of the bush between Lind's and I and Todd below us. The head belonged to a very inquisitive Brown Bear that was spying my wife and bouncing his head up and down trying his hardest to get a sniff of what she was.

I somewhat calmly yelled to our team, "We have a Bear" right here" Most concerned about Todd since he was between us and our bear spray and the bear. The bear hadn't suspected Todd, and Todd hadn't noticed the bear. Todd, got a little too excited and pretty much ran out into the water. It looked like he had wadable water all the way across....but between his splashing and my yelling our brown furry friend stepped out of the brush and now was paying all of his attention to Lindsay and I. I had started into my yelling of "Hey we are fishing here...get the fuck away from us" rant, but now that I had a full view of this bruin...I became even more worried. He wasn't that big as in maybe a two year old cub. Big enough to create a lot of harm to any of us, but my concern was if his mother the Sow was still in the picture, and was she nearby and alerted to this commotion?

Lindsay and the other Dave backed up the trail while the bear and I continued our standoff. And it was just that. Unlike my other encounters where at my initial rant the bears ran off, this one wasn't leaving. Todd meanwhile had navigated himself across the river, but he was all by himself, and no bear spray. Behind Todd was some thick brush and forest which easily could contain more bears.

This bear stared at me.....stood his ground, and didn't flinch. The bears in this part of Alaska see lots of tourists. My mind was racing, and for good measure I had un-holstered the Bear Spray. While I have read scores of articles on the effectiveness of Bear Spray, I had ZERO confidence this was going to stop this animal should he decide to shut my big mouth. But once again....while I was acting very agitated...I felt calm inside, I was two for two batting 1000 in two previous very close encounters with these guys, why it didn't occur to me that you can't ever stay at 1000%....I mean Ted Williams the best hitter in baseball only batted over 400 ...ONCE!

The bear started to circle from his stance. My main concern was not pushing him down stream towards Todd and not letting him go up the trail that would lead him to Dave and Lindsay. He was headed towards the trail that led him to Lindsay and Dave, so I also started moving to cut him off all the while making a ton of racket and getting as big and angry as I could.

I stopped his advance towards the trail up stream, he acted like he could care less what I had to say, and then to all of our relief slowly and deliberately climbed up the steep bank and as easy as walking through an open field, slipped through the alders and bramble as if it wasn't even there. I remember even before my relief that he was leaving hit me, I was astonished how easily something that big could traipse through that thick jungle without being snagged. He never broke stride.

We all regained our composure. Here we had spent most of the day in the high country, not seeing another human being or bear all day, now we're down where there were plenty of other anglers mill-ing around, and we run into a bear in a manner that one would come across another fisherman. First decision was not to climb the stairs to the parking lot near where the bear had walked out. But to instead hike back up the trail and take the next walk out.

Before we left, I had to know. I had to know how close this animal was when he first appeared. I walked it off.....22 feet.

8

Out Numbered By The Fairer Sex In Alaska

THERE IS NO one luckier on this planet, at winning raffles and drawings than my wife Lindsay. Two years ago at the Spey Nation Clave on New York's Salmon River, as they got down to the two final drawings. One a trip to BC, the other a trip to Alaska, and with Lindsay in both buckets... .I just knew we'd win one.

Both of us have fished Alaska many times (as evidences by the other offerings in my Alaska Chronicles), so I was hoping for BC. The Alaska trip was for several days free guided trips on the Kenai Peninsula. Again since we had fished it many times, winning that would be OK, because when not being guided at no charge, we knew many other rivers and creeks to fish on our own. But was still hoping for the Skeena Trip to BC.

As her luck would have it they announced Lindsay's name on the Alaska Trip bucket pull. The place went crazy, and many other players for the two grand prizes were heard mumbling in the background that Lindsay winning anything was NOT a surprise. And many congratulated her.

Fast forward a year later when we could actually fit this trip in, and besides the three guided days free, I had enough Alaska Air miles from my AA credit card to fly virtually free for the both of us. We have two very good friends Lisa and Terri, who started fly fishing a few years ago, and hinted they'd like to tag along…if we could work something out with the free guided days. I contacted the guide who offered the trip, and he said he could take four, and he would charge the other two ladies his regular per person fee, and of course Lind's and I would be providing a generous tip each day, so by adding in Lisa and Terri, this was a win win for everybody.

As mentioned in many of my writing about trips, planning and anticipating the trips are nearly as exciting as going on the trip. The four of us talked about timing of the trip, and we decided a fall trip would be best as we were truly all interested in Rainbows and Dolly Varden, hoping to mix in some late run Silvers. The March before our Sept. 10 departure Lisa and I coordinated a side by side booking of flights so we could make sure we all flew together to and from Anchorage. The one minor hitch was flights were much better (Lisa had an Alaska Air Card as well, and had the same deal for flight costs) from Buffalo NY VS our home town of Rochester. But Lind's and I had done the trip from Buffalo before. A 45 minute ride down the highway, stay overnight across from the airport leave my truck right at the hotel and get the shuttle to the front door…easy peasy.

As the date of the trip neared, all four of us got together a few times to lock down our plans for travel, fishing and site seeing as a basic itinerary. Lisa had been to the Great State to get on a cruise ship out of Seward, but hadn't been down to the Peninsula at Homer. And we anticipated the many other creeks we would fish beside the Kenai with the guides. Lisa had done the deep dive on places to stay and our intel was to make base camp in Coopers Landing and fish up and down the river from there. She found a wonderful Cabin on a rise above the Kenai River, run by couple who were true Alaskan Dog Sleder's with 15 to 20 dogs and houses about the property. The cabin was perfect, warm cozy with all the comforts of home.

Flying from the east coast to Anchorage (which I've done nearly 10 times) is an all-day grueling affair. I guess Lindsay and I are still a tad bit gun shy of Airlines losing our gear, so we strap on a couple backpacks with waders, boots, a change of clothing, rods, reels and flies as carry-ons. Lisa and Terri followed suit, and there was no mistaking us for casual travelers in the airports we visited to and from.

The night before a trip and in this case starting out of town it's fun to go out and have a nice dinner. We checked into the hotel, after some scrambling when Lisa discovered we had booked the overnight the day before our actual arrival...and we quickly got it squared away. Asked the front desk for a decent dinner choice. They provided a tavern combination Micro Brewery about 10 minutes away. I'm a stickler for getting a trip off on the right foot, and this recommendation was spot on. Food was great, beer was very good.

Wake up was at O dark 30, and we mustered in the lobby to catch the shuttle across the street. Probably could have gotten a little later start, but I guess the adrenalin was pumping in all four of us. I'm of the mindset that once you step on an airplane be it a jumbo jet, or a Beaver on a lake or river, they shut the doors, and the Pilot fires up he bird, I'm good with trusting them. They don't want to die either. The flights were fairly non impactful. A few bumps in the air, Every plane was full, except the first leg, and as we flew into the Alaskan Mountain range we had clear blue skies so one could view the immense vastness from the air.

On the ground all the bags and gear accounted for, the rental Van was quick and easy again thanks to Lisa's preemptive planning...we were on our way to Dee's to spend the night in Anchorage before heading down south to fish. OK to that point it was all good. Until I made the girls follow my tradition of having dinner upon arrival at the Blue Fox. My girl buddy Mandy was still tending bar there five years later since our last visit, BUT the place had seen better days, and they were in between Chefs. The girls passed on the food...and while I ate... nobody was buying into my rave that this place had some yummy eats.

Dee and her husband Yves used to own and run the Alaska House of Jade B&B. The new owner didn't have a vacancy but knew I was a longtime customer and told me Dee had a condo and still handled some guests. So we got to spend the first night at Dee's have a scotch, tell a few stories get a great night sleep, and most of all Dee's fabulous breakfast to start our day the next morning.

The ride down to Coopers Landing through the Turnagain Arm even on a rainy day is nothing less than spectacular. We stopped several times for the girls to get some pictures. Plans were since we couldn't check in to the cabin until 3 PM, and it was before noon, we'd head over to Ptarmigan Creek which drains into Kenai Lake in hopes of finding some spawning Sockeye. Finding red salmon usually resulted in Rainbows and Dolly Varden trailing their flanks to vacuum up the nutritious eggs.

Lind's and I were rigged up pretty quickly. This is a small trib width wise so easy to fish in most places. As I rounded the corner taking a glance at the water before suiting up, I saw what I was looking for. Spawning reds on gravel. Moments later Lind's and I had wadded into position and it wasn't long before we each kicked off the trip with some pretty olive, silver pink spotted Dolly's to hand. These fish were relatively smaller, but feisty none the less. Lisa and Terri joined in, and landed some pretty fish. We spent a couple hours catching these spunky Char until it was near time to head to the cabin.

The cabin was wonderful. Plenty of space, warm and cozy. After unloading our gear, we took a ride down to Coppers Landing's main drag to a few fly and tackle shops, grocery stores and tourist attractions from panning for gold shops, to trinket shops. We all picked up a few clothing items that had the local logos of Alaska and fishing and headed out for a bite to eat.

Monday morning we were to meet Guide Eric down in town. Day one was a ride across Skilak Lake to the tail out of the upper Kenai river in hopes of finding Char and rainbows....maybe even a few silvers. All through the night the wind was a gale with heavy rain and we wondered how rough the lake was. We got to the launch at Skilak Lake and there were two boats hovering near the launch ramp. The lake was rolling but didn't look to bad. Looks like these two boats are coming in, not leaving.

And they were. They had gone out the day before to fish the same area we were headed to. They made the mistake after beaching their boats and staying too long to where when the wind came up, they couldn't get their boats off shore and had to spend the night in the pouring rain and cold on the shore line until the wind died and they could get off the beach. They looked a little haggard, but one of the boats had a full canvas top so we assumed they all huddled under it for the night. BUT, they didn't seem worse for wear, and the reason they got caught out was the fishing was so spectacular, they couldn't pull away in time to get back home.

Eric got the rods and boat rigged, and chatted with the once stranded crew. They noted that once around the point, the lake was pretty "Sporty" . Now having guided on the Great Lakes for over 2 decades, in both boats the size of Eric's and much bigger I know what Sporty means. I have to stop here and applaud my girl crew. They had the right foul weather gear for the job, and while I'm sure we all had a few anxious moments on the cross to the river tail-out, they were tough and determined. Eric admitted later that had we encountered the roughest water sooner in the cross, he would have turned around. But we were within a few hundred yards of the beaching when we hit the really nasty rollers, and I would agree it would have probably been worse to turn around at that point to fight our way back.

Batten Down the Hatches

We pulled up on a gravel bar, shook like dogs getting out of a lake, checked to see if we had all our parts and pieces, and commenced to fishing. As usual Lindsay stepped out of the boat, made a cast and caught a pretty Dolly. We spread out along this gravel bar, with plenty of Sockeye in front of us, picked out a pack of them, and dropped our egg patterns behind them, hooking up time after time. I got a hard tug and landed a hard fighting Dolly in the low 20 inch range. Looking down the line, all the ladies continued to hook up.

One of dozens of big Dolly's on the Upper Kenai

Not being one to stand in one spot for too long, I did a little search-ing up the run. I settled into a nice spot, made a cast, and my 10 foot 7 Wt., with the noisy Hardy Salmon click and pawl started to buck and squeal to a mid-20's rainbow who had eaten the fly, and was grey hounding away from me at light speed. Into my backing I began to chase him down river. A couple more jumps, but I got square with him, and then just below, and finally inched him into the net. Beautiful Kenai River bow of about 26 inches.

The Leopards of Alaska

The catching went on for the better part of an hour or so, when Eric said, let's check out this back channel. It's usually holding bigger fish. We had to get back in the boat and round the point to access the back channel. Loaded up, we bucked a few nasty rollers and glided into a slot off the main lake that looked like a dead end. Once anchored to a tree to hold the boat, we followed a small trail into a flow that could have been a river all its own, but was simply a braid off the main Upper Kenai.

A nice long shallow gravel bar awaited us, and we spread out again with hundreds of Sockeye in view. Lind's and I leap frogged our way up stream, taking fish after fish mostly Dollies, and some very pretty rainbows. This braid was wadable to the middle so we could hit the deeper slot on the far bank, and were rewarded with what Eric brought us here for, most fish in the low to mid 20 inch range. Hard fighting and sometimes aerial Dollies. Terri and Lisa were holding down the fort below us, and even found a few big Sockeye that decided their egg flies were a nuisance.

With over an hour left to fish, Lindsay and I were exhausted from catching fish, so we broke down our rods, sat on a nearby hummock and watched Terri and Lisa finish off the day. Out of the hide away slot back into the big lake we had a couple cold nasty breakers over the bow. But in no more then two minutes we had the right angle from the waves to make the ride back to the launch pleasurable. A full day one of fishing in the books, and we had all caught dozens of beautiful wild Alaska trout and salmon.

Had to include a shot of Lindsay's trend setting RED fishing nails

Our Itinerary for Tuesday was to head to Homer. The plans were decided due to the weather forecasts. It was going to be a spectacular sunny day, and when descending into Homer down to the famous Spit of land with saloons, shops and restaurants, if you can do it on a sunny day you get the spectacular view of the Kenai mountain range. Ahh but fishing was on the plans as well. Deep Creek and the Anchor river were reported to be enjoying a fine run of Steelhead. Anytime you can have a shot at fresh ocean run rainbows you do your best to get a shot at them. It's funny how the Seward to Homer section of Alaska works. It can be sunny in Soldotna, and Cooper Landing, and raining in Seward and Homer. The mountain ranges dictate the weather that swirls around them. So as we rolled into both Deep Creek and the Anchor, we were met with rushing high off color water. A stop at the local fly shop in Anchor Point dropped your chin another level lower when the shop owner tells you the Anchor has one of the best runs of steelhead in years...and on Sat (three days ago) when it was fishing really well many fish in the mid-teens pounds wise were caught.

We stopped at a couple put in points on the Anchor River, but it was evident it was rolling high hard and dirty and wading would be a dangerous adventure. After a long tiring escapade of fish on the Kenai less than 24 hours ago, we decided a day of sightseeing in Homer was in order. With its massive harbor, cradling everything from small fishing skiffs to some of Deadliest Catch's Crab fleet, Lind's and I could wander around there all day. We hit all the shops at the Spit, and then Lind's and I took Lisa and Terri to our favorite place for lunch at the very end of the Spit. The Land's End Resort. Here you can get the freshest Halibut sandwich in Alaska with fresh fish arriving hourly from commercial and sport fishing boats. And the lunch didn't disappoint nor did the wild life right out the restaurant window, of sea lions, sea otters, eagles, and the breath taking mountain rage fully visible on this clear blue sky day.

Day three would be DIYER fishing the Russian River. We found a good parking area in the State Park in which to traverse down to the river. Now both Terri and Lisa wanted to see an Alaskan Brown Bear in the wild, not to close. Refer to my "Playing Nicely with Bears" essay and you'll remember we had our "closest" encounter with a Brown Bear right here on the Russian River. And I was a tad nervous fishing with three ladies, because I know the Bears scent the ladies easily and get curious.

As we got to the river course it was evident of two things. The Sockeyes were all but done in this river which was key for maybe not running into a bear, but also meant the Rainbows and Dollies would not be schooled up as easy targets behind the salmon. And the River was very low. So we hiked up River looking for a pod of Red's and or some deeper slots that would hold fish, and after an hour or so we were striking out. Our only recourse was to hike back to the confluence of the Russian River as it merged in with the Kenai. We fished the gravel bars for a while, having some success, but not much.

We also had planned to hit Seward this day after fishing, and decided we'd head there earlier than planned due to the slow fishing and imperfect conditions. Lind's and I've been to Seward probably five times. Nothing new going on there, same shops in the same places, fresh halibut lunch there as well. Lisa and Terri had not been there, so this visit was more interesting for them. Lind's and I were burning to get back on the water while Lisa and Terri wanted to visit the Glacier nearby.

Lisa offered to run us back to Ptarmigan Creek, double back to the Glacier, and then pick us up on the way home. Truly was a lot of driving, but a shot to get the last few hours on the water, Lind's and I hoped in our waders...so we could jettison out of the van in the creek parking area. I'd drive us to the creek, and then Lisa would take over.

I was a little too anxious to get out of the Seward City limits, and soon there was flashing lights on my tail, and of course I was cursing out loud, for being stupid and in a hurry. The Alaska State Trooper cautiously slid alongside the driver's door. He had already found the Van on his computer and knew it was rented. No telling what these out of towners were up to in a rented Van. When he was sure it was safe. He started the standard license registration and rental agreement request, but stopped mid-sentence. Noticing Lind's and I in waders....the Trooper said...hey you going fishing, to which we replied yes, we're fly fishermen heading back down to Ptarmigan Creek. He said "I was out yesterday and got some nice Bows and Dollies" and in the process produced some cell phone pictures, for which I in return followed suit with my cell phone. The next five minutes were spent talking fly fishing, and different rivers in the area, and he finally said, "Hey, look I'm not going to write you a ticket, but please slow down and take it easy".

Sure enough officer, and we were back on the road. Lind's and I caught some pretty fish in the stream, Lisa and Terri got a look at the Glacier, and I escaped what was probably $100 fine for speeding or worse simply because I had my waders on.

Thursday we had a paid for guide trip with one of my favorite outfitters in Cooper Landing, Tom Lassard. Tom has Cabins right on the river and does float trips in the upper Kenai. This day we had one of his guide staff Chad. Chad was your typical late 30's early 40's guide who had grown up out west some place. Was never the kind of guy who wanted to sit in an office, could kill a moose, guide fishermen, and of course was a carpenter skilled tradesman for the off season work to be able to stay liquid enough living in the Alaska. Chad was methodical, he didn't know our capabilities and had to assess if the four of us could fly fish from a drift boat. So we anchored up mid river, and practiced casting our Indy Rigs in rhythm to not tangle or hook each other. Chad was satisfied that his crew for the day likely wouldn't hook each other, and especially him, we started the drift.

Terri and Lisa didn't have much experience fly casting, mending line and controlling their drift from a moving boat, but they caught on quickly and soon everyone was into hard fighting jumping Alaskan Rainbows, and Dollies. Several stops along the way to fish likely gravel bars and each one held a number of fish. One stop Lindsay waded down to the tail out. After catching at least 8 fish in eight successive casts invited Terri to take her place and Terri never skipped a beat and continued the consecutive cast and catch run. Lisa and I both hooked and landed several large Bows. We fished a chute that swung behind the gravel bar and dumped back into the river proper after rolling past a few tress that provided cover in a deeper hole along the bank.

This day was bright and Sunny and as the day grew longer we were all shedding our layers of foul weather gear and it became down right balmy to where I was fishing in short sleeves. You could tell Chad was relieved to have four anglers who could get the job done but true to having guided countless parties where some or all were beginners Chad couldn't help himself early on to coach our every move. After a while he came to me to apologize for all the coaching when it was evident we didn't require that much attention, but my rule of thumb with guides, is they are the boss, run their game, their process, and if they figure out we don't need as much hand holding that's good. But honestly I always learn something new from all the guides I've used.

Another day where the four of us together easily landed more fish than you could count. Tired but happy we bid Chad farewell. Our favorite place to eat in Coopers Landing is a Roadside tavern that doesn't look like much from the road called the King Fisher Roadhouse. The young gal that owns and is the head Chef has an amazing talent from appetizers, like fresh Halibut Nachos, to her Elk Stew, and her steaks were meats that were aged and seasoned to perfection. BUT, the best of all is her Key Lime pie. Yeah I know you're tilting you head...huh what...Key Lime Pie in Alaska, not the Florida Keys...no way....I'm telling you ...WAY! As we were leaving, I saw Chad our guide at the bar, and we stopped to say hi, and left another extra tip to buy he and his friends a few rounds of the Alaskan Brown.

We still had two more free to Lind's and I anyway guided trips with Eric. We hit the middle part of the Kenai both days fishing from the boat. It was anticlimactic at best. The fishing is stupid easy. But there was one slight tragedy on that Saturday trip. Lisa had just landed ANOTHER nice fish. Eric popped the hook and tossed the fly over the side. Before Lisa could pick up her rod, another fish grabbed her fly and launched her fly rod and reel out of the boat. Lindsay standing nearby frantically started casting in the direction it was last seen to no avail.

A minute or so later it popped straight up out of the water but we were too far away to try and net or hook it. And then it disappeared. Forever. Lisa was not happy, and you can't blame her. We had other rods, but you can never be overly content as good as the fishing was for losing a nice fly rod and reel. The boat fell silent in mourning for the rod. Me being a world class ball buster sat there pulling back on the reins. I kept looking at Eric our guide. I could tell the little twitch he had going, he was holding back as well. Finally I couldn't stand it any longer. "Lisa, you should be glad you're of the fairer sex. Cause if this was a boat full of guys the ball busting right now would be merciless. And as I said that Eric couldn't help himself..."oh yeah Lisa, we'd be saying all kinds of shit...Ohh Hey is that you rod over there, wait I think I see it." Lisa might find that banter funnier today.. but not so much at that moment.

The last day of our trip, we had to drive back to Anchorage to catch a late day flight. No need to jump out of bed this day since we weren't going fishing. But as usual my internal alarm clock is ringing at 5 bells. I quietly as I can slip out of bed, take a shower and decide to run down to the fly shop in town to maybe pick up a few other T-Shirts etc. I do that, then feeling hungry step into the General Store that is a combination gas station, hunting and fishing, grocery store, diner. I order up some breakfast and the nice lady behind the counter says go on out into the dining area, I'll bring your order out to you when its ready. I walk into this little eating area, with maybe five tables, and sitting in eight of the 10 available seats are a group of "Alaskan Men". I'm not talking right out of some TV reality show, I mean bearded burly mountain men strapped down with their .44s talking MONEY and POLITICS.

I stopped them in the middle of their conversation. Gentlemen, I've just spent a week fishing with three of the Fairer Sex, and I'm in desperate need of some testosterone, so keep talking Money, Politics, Hunting and Fishing, and I'll just sit here and let that talk waif over me. They laughed and we had a fun conversation. On the way back to the cabin, what walks out in front of me....a Huge Sow Brown Bear and two Cubs, not 200 yards from the cabin. Since we had not come across any bears on this trip, which was the first time ever for me, I almost didn't have the heart to tell Terri who was still hoping to see a live bear in the wild ..and not behind bars at the zoo.

*She may have lost a Fly Rod, but she didn't
lose many fish...Lisa with a trophy.*

9

The Haunting

THE HERITAGE OF fishing includes at least ONE fish in your life time that you did not land, the proverbial "One That Got Away". This is usually a fish you are specifically targeting, many times have planned a special trip for, and had your moment with that fish a near miss and a fish story for a lifetime.

I was on such a trip, and yes I was targeting a particular fish, in this case Atlantic Salmon, but not in one of the romantic settings that is the heritage of Atlantic Salmon as in the Gaspe' Peninsula, Norway, Russia, Iceland or the British Isles. No these were Great Lakes Landlocked Atlantic Salmon, hatchery raised fish, (any snobby purist Atlantic Salmon Angler can stop reading now). And the place was not set in the magical background of the afore mentioned locations. Instead I was standing in the St. Mary's Rapids, in Sault Saint Marie Canada, staring over to the US side of the river at the locks that oil tankers, grain carriers and iron ore ships used to move in and out of Lake Superior.

But the Rapids themselves are mind blowing, with a current running about 5 knots out of the gates at the Dam, tumbling over a half mile wide series of boulders creating infinite chutes, seams, syrup like glassy pools, and frothy fast runs. Pocket water galore. The Salmon come into this flow from Lake Huron to spawn. Many swim right back to the Power House on the US side where Roger Greil a professor and fisheries biologist working at Lake Superior State University created this phenomena spawns them..

Charlie, Fran, and Keld are experienced Salmon Anglers who have fished for pure strain ocean fish in many of the places listed above including Russia. We had made the 12 hour drive from my house in Western NY two days before, and had limited success in catching some of these fish. Keld and I had each brought two grilse to hand between 8 and 12 pounds. Fran and Charlie had some action as well, but it was by no means fast and furious. Fishing the long two handed rods, and swinging streamers on floating lines we had raised few fish in two full days of fishing. I, being the least experienced had proven that fishing can be a lot about luck sometimes, besides the two landed, I had three other fish come to my flies. Charlie likes to keep track of high rod as a joke or a method, mainly because he follows up the high rod finalist as the person who's digging deepest in his pockets to buy rounds in the pub.

First Soo Salmo Salar with guide John Giuliani

It was the last evening of our trip, late June, and it was abnormally hot and humid in the Soo. So our method of chasing these fish was early morning until the Sun got high and the temperature ascended to the muggy stage which was about 10 AM. Go back to the motel, get a late breakfast or early lunch in town, maybe siesta then back at it after 5 PM until dark. Finish the night at the "Dock", a fine restaurant on the river for great food. This place had a chef that prepared delicious dishes couple with tall frosty pints of Rickards Red a premium brew the Dock had on tap.

Outside of fishing from a boat in the two power house pools, there was a small platform, and shore line in the Canadian Power house pool you could fish from shore and then about a mile of Rapids. The Rapids I have failed to mention are treacherous. I covered the current at an honest 5 to 7 knots, the boulders were the size of Volkswagens or bowling balls, neither are conducive for easy wading. So you had to pick your way along in the current. Let it be known, you can wade from the Canadian shore to the US shore, but it's truly dangerous.

It's Friday evening, about 6 PM...we've decided to split up. Keld and I are going into the rapids, while Fran and Charlie fish the Canadian power house pool from shore. The salmon have two main sources of energy in the St. Mary's. Lake smelt that are available everywhere, and the largest caddis hatches I've ever seen. There is a Hex hatch as well but normally in July. I had all my action so far on a simple J-Hook size six or four cone head muddler in a bone or off-white tie, and an Olive tie. The day before I had fished down a cement berm that parallels the river. You walk the berm, find a slice of water you want to fish, and you can safely wade to, jump off the berm and pick your way to the river.

The day before I had hit a couple of these pools and runs, and I had a hard tug in a little drop pool in the slick at the tail just as the river rushed down a chute to the next slick. I had left Keld in the locally famous Canadian Pool where we had both picked up three of the four fish between us...jumped up on the ledge and started walking. My first stop was at the pool I had raised the fish the day before. Once I was set up in a good foot hold, I proceeded to launch a series of casts from near to mid, and far side of the pool and let the fly make its journey from the top of the run, to the bottom. This assault only lasted about 20 minutes and I decided to move. I hadn't been down river much further then this spot, but I had spied a glassy pool at the end of the wall, and had yet to fish it. Being the last night, my intentions were to end the trip there. It's was about 6:15, and I had to pick my way back up to the Berm, to descend to my next target. Had I tried to wade down, the time in which to make that wade would have exceeded the daylight left to get there. Probably 50 yards with over an hour and a half left of day light. That's how treacherous the SOO can be.

Hopped off the Berm at my final destination. I couldn't see Keld way up river, and I was the only soul down there. In fact I was willing to bet nobody had fished this spot that day. As I arrived at the head of this run, it was spectacular. 90 to 100 foot wide. The far side was a fast riffle with a distinct seam folding into the glassy syrup . The "Syrup" was about 70 foot in width of this run, and it narrowed at the tail as it rocketed into the next descending chute to about 40 feet across. The near side was a seam much like the far seam. This pool was in a pure bracket of fast roily water. Many of you reading this have had this feeling. The minute I got my foot hold and was ready to cast, I heard myself say it aloud, there is going to be a fish in here. You couldn't dream or draw up a more perfect lie for a Salmon.

I remember hesitating for an instant to coach myself, NOT to fire all the way across on the first cast even though I could picture in my mind's eye, right where the fish should be holding. The water in the Rapids is crystal clear...and I could see the edge of this pool drop out of sight, so this target had everything. Lots of oxygen, depth to protect the fish from the SUN and predators, breaks and eddies at the head and tail that would trap bait fish and aquatics. This was a Salmon's nirvana. So with discipline, I worked the fly through the near seam just in case the fish I knew would be there had been located in that perfect lie. Not a touch. I plied the middle of the pool and still nothing. I was working about 70 feet of line, and while I should have stripped out another 10 to 20 feet and hit the third quarter of this run, my discipline ran out, and I stripped out the line I'd need to reach across the 100 foot seam on the other side. I had been using a 540 grain Vision Scandi head custom made at the Deschutes Angler on a 14 foot Talon custom blank that a good friend had built for me earlier that year. Snap T … formed the D loop and let it fly, like a golfer hitting the sweet spot on his Big Bertha driver…I felt the line and rod in harmony, and the fly shot true to the far edge of the roily seam. Now this is NOT a fish story, I'm telling you exactly what was going through my mind, I knew on that cast if there was a fish in here, this was it, this was the special delivery the fish was waiting for. What I'm saying is I knew I was about to get bit.

Now once in a while in a person's life you reach perfection in the realm of poetic justice. Poetic justice was if I was designing this about to happen scenario, I would want the fish to take HARD, be angry as hell, run and jump several times, and smile for the camera as I was snapping his picture. I had come all this way, I had waded gingerly in this vast mine field of boulders and slippery snot to reach this pool, Justice Must be Served.

THE TUG was vicious, and I yelled out load to nobody "HERE WE GO"….This fish didn't come all the way out of the water, but thrashed to the surface it's head out of the water, and then slapped it's tail in the glassy film, I remember how high the spray jumped from this first angry reaction, and quickly my mind started running dimensions from the head, tail and amount of spray to spit out an answer, this is the biggest fish I've hooked or seen all week.

The fish immediately pivoted from north to south and stampeded out of the run and down into the froth at the tail, my heart sank as there was NO WAY I could chase this fish, and the reel was humming the fishes departure music. I mentioned I was a greenhorn at this salmon game, but with a 12 hour ride to get to this place, I had taken the opportunity to pick the brain of the Mad Dane, or rather the Danish Viking about Atlantic Salmon. Keld was much obliged to fill all 12 hours with stories, antidotes, and advice about these wonderful fish. One fact stuck in my craw, Atlantic Salmon don't actually LIKE to leave the pool. So if you take pressure off them, many times they will return to the pool you hooked them in. The fish had stopped down in the fast water, and I quickly stripped two pulls of line to take all the pressure off the fish, hoping the iron was locked in....and just like out of the "Book of Keld", the salmon swam back into the pool. I reeled in the slack, and got a good bend back in the 14 footer and as expected ticked Mr. Salmon off a second time. This time he took to the air, and I finally got my first look at him, and he was easily well over 30 inches, and pure silver. He crashed to the water whipping up a second waterfall of spray and headed down stream again. I adjusted the drag and slowed him down, rolled the rod downstream and once again he swam to me.

I now had him 30 feet from my boots, I'll never forget this, he acted like a puppy on a leash. He was wagging back and forth in the current facing me head down, and I wasn't really pulling on him that much. Instead I had turned my attention to a landing zone. About 10 yards away was a little side channel that looked to have gravel in it, which would give me good footing to capture him and snap a quick picture. I would lay my rod alongside him for scale of measurement because the boys were going to get a kick out of this. So the fish is at a 45 degree angle down stream of me, but he's not up on his side, he's just hanging down there....Pump and reel, Pump and reel, he's 10 feet off the tip of the rod...he's mine, what a way to end the trip...fish of a life time for me, man that Rickards Red is going to taste really good....I might have two or 10 to celebrate.....and then it all came undone. The Poetic Justice I was leaning on fell over and me with it.

The fish made a left hand turn up into the current, and with one swoosh of his mighty tail was eight feet in the air, before I knew what was happening he's airborne a second, third and fourth time, meanwhile the rush of water near my position had caught and buried the Skandi head in the flow, and I couldn't get the head out of the current to turn the rod towards the fish. So my rod is pointing downstream, the shooting head is buried in the flow, meanwhile on jump number four where I'm looking to the heavens as if gazing at the stars that will be out soon. I'm looking over my shoulder while facing downstream at this Manic fish "Up Stream". He just hung there like Jordan gliding to the basket from the foul line,....and on that fourth launch with my rod tip under water....I heard the ping of the 14 pound tippet, and my fly and the fish were gone.

There had been a crescendo in my head all through this fight, a mighty orchestra was playing with Vigor, the 1812 Overture. And now the stage was empty, the only sound was the water rushing over my boots ...and the din of a seagull in the distance, either laughing or crying for me...but probably laughing since I would expect all the animal kingdom roots for its own.

I was trembling, and I started to smile, then I started to laugh, shaking my head, smiling from ear to ear, as if I had actually closed the deal. While I had caught two of these wonderful fish, and the fight from both was memorable, I had just been dunked in baptism for what these fish were all about. I had been given a greater gift then a picture of a fish next to a rod. I instead, had been exposed to the lethal love potion that thousands before me had experienced, the power, the beauty, the majesty of a creature that could execute ridiculous tactics to escape, yet on his way back to the water make you feel like you had completed the deal, win isn't the correct term ...because the fish won. However we had a relationship that I'll never relinquish unless or until I lose my mind. In that brief encounter my veins filled with the exuberance and passion to do "THAT" again...or in other words continue trying to catch Atlantic Salmon.

I sat on a boulder, the time was a little after 8 PM. It would be dark in less than an hour, and I had a semi difficult hike back to Keld, and then to Charlie and Fran. It was a beautiful sun setting, I just couldn't stop smiling, I had never experienced such an absolute bombastic fish like this one. Finally, I rose from the rock, and made my way to the Berm and back to fetch Keld. Telling Keld of my experience was anticlimactic, because he's caught so many Atlantic Salmon he always had one better, but I thanked him for the important tip on taking pressure off the fish so he woudn't leave the pool.

We snaked our way back through the forested path to the parking lot, and walked down to the Power House area where the truck was parked. Keld and I didn't discuss the fish much longer likely because I was in shock, however my friend Charlie, who has a sixth sense, knew the moment he saw me, that I had been spooked. I was really past normal ear shot ...when I tried to speak, my mouth was moving, and some gibberish was coming out, but my mind and mouth were not in sync. I was stuttering and waving my arms, and not making any sense. Charlie and Fran got it...they understood...I'd been bitten by the beast. I would never be the same again.

Dr. Blaas (Charlie) is an absolute Hall Of Fame.. Ball Buster. If you have a humbling experience and Charlie gets wind of it...or worse yet experiences with you he feels it's his duty to relive this moment with you and in front of strangers for the rest of time. So the more frantic I got reliving my story, the more Charlie would egg me on to give him more data, more facts, on the undressing that a fish had just given me. At that moment I was a total sappy mess, blabbering all over myself and it continued into the Dock at the bar as I obliged to be the buyer of the divine Rickards Reds brews for having the best fish story.

One of the best things that have come out of this story is the re-telling of it. Now very seldom have I orchestrated the retelling. I'm fortunate to be on rivers with my buddy Charlie. Charlie is the un-spoken Mayor at many of these rivers. Mid-day usually finds Charlie and another gentlemen or two on the river to strike up a conversation while he enjoys his standard Monte Cristo. Charlie is a master at the philosophical dissection of any individual he meets while fishing. Trade some pleasantries and the conversation always delves into where this new acquaintance likes to fish and what for. Then he works into the soup he's cooking past trips and adventures. He times this right as he brings these conversations to a slow boil by mixing in the last ingredient....ME.

He takes the listener to the Soo, the majestic dangerous St Mary's Rapids, and then introduces the "haunting" his friend had there. He times this as I'm catching up to him, or taking a break and joining him on the bank and then he simply ally oops the ball to me as I'm breaking to the basket, and I finish the deposition in my still haunted frame of mind and slam dunk the listener into this adventure. All the while Dr. Blaas puffs away on the Monte....smiling, and adding color commentary and background like a perfect rock drummer filling in the guitar riffs of a classic rock song.

10

Keeler Fly

ONE OF THE most enjoyable aspects of fly fishing is the tying of flies and then having fish eat your own creations. I have been tying flies for a long time. I have saved some of my first flies, and it's funny as in embarrassing to look at them so many years later. But one thing remains even if you've become a better fly tier, Crappy flies still catch fish.

Lindsay and I have made several trips, day trips, weekend trips, week long jaunts to places like Alaska, but we had never ventured to the Salt water. We live less than a day's drive from Long Island Sound and Martha's Vineyard, but we decided to leap all the way to wading a Bonefish flat in the Mexican Caribbean. We'd never fished for bonefish before, knew only what we had watched for years on Saturday morning TV fishing shows. We talked to some outfitters at the Somerset Fly Fishing show in New Jersey, and settled on a quaint little lodge operation in Ascension Bay.

Why Mexico? Because my research yielded the perception (at least) that Mexico Bonefish were easier than their Bahamian cousins. Since this was our first dance, we decided to find the most illiterate bonefish we could find. In the end the Bones of Mexico aren't illiterate, they just don't see as many flies as the Bonefish of the Keys or Bahamas and provide a situation that allows for a few more mistakes then other places.

This was 2007.....and we had planned an early November trip hopefully after hurricane season. That September as I was monitoring the hurricane movements on the internet, I started watching hurricane Dean. And to my horror Dean rolled around in the Gulf for a bit and then took aim at you guessed it. Ascension Bay and came right down the throat of Pesca Maya Lodge. My first concern was for the tiny villages in that area, as this location is very rural. We received the news that several of the beautiful native style huts at the lodge had been damaged beyond use, yet the Lodge was still open for business and Dean hadn't ruined the flats around this area. Closest we had ever come to truly using our trip insurance.

Time to travel, and we arrive in Cancun to the wonderful warm relief from the cold weather we'd left in Upstate New York. The process is to get through customs, walk outside and somebody with a sign reading "Dave and Lindsay" or "Pesca Maya" would be on the sidewalk waiting for us. But first we had to almost live through a girl's WORST nightmare. We had a one hop flight to Cancun. Rochester to Charlotte, then Charlotte to our final destination. We had plenty of layover time in Charlotte so the last thing we worried about was losing our luggage. Of course the rods reels and flies were carry on, so even if we didn't have a change of cloths we could fish. At the baggage claim, my bag tumbled down the chute and we patiently waited for Lindsay's. And waited and waited. Frustrated we determined somehow her stuff was lost, so we looked around for the lost claims baggage stand or office. Suddenly, a garage door cranked open near the baggage dock and one lone bag was pushed through by a handler, and then he closed the door...not a group of bags...ONE BAG...and it was Lindsay's.

So far we had dodged the Dean Hurricane bullet, and now the lost luggage possible fiasco. Waltzed through customs, and out into the bright warm Caribbean sunlight. We looked for our names on a sign or Pesca Maya signs, hats anything, nothing, so we started asking around and sure enough a very pleasant man named Felix stepped up and said I'm here to drive you to the Lodge.

The very first thing that Felix does after loading our gear in his jeep, is to swing into the Beverage store. Felix asked us what we'd like to drink? We chose water and beer for the four hour drive. Things were looking up one after another. The drive is along the Ocean, through several high end resort areas until you get into the Sian Ka'an Eco System Park, then becomes a bumpy dirt road for close to two hours. Just before we hit the dirt roads, we stopped at a little outdoor Taco stand and dined on fresh homemade Taco's filled with meats and shrimp. A cold Cerveza, and then the second leg of the trip began.

About an hour down the dirt highway, some locals were out on the road and waving Felix down. Felix obliged and pulled over. I could tell from the excited tone and rapid fire language something was urgent. Off to our left a group of people emerged from the bush, they looked tired, and haggard. Felix got on his cell phone made a call...spoke to the other party on the phone, shook hands with the local villagers and jumped back in the jeep and we were off again. Felix explained the folks who came out of the jungle were Cubans who had floated in on a home-made raft. This happens all the time in this part of Mexico. The process is to call the police. The Police come and pick the refugees up, and take them to a camp, where they are treated by local doctors and brought back to good health, and then they work through the legal system to get Visa's and Felix admitted many continue on trying to get to the US.

OK so not your typical arrival to your fishing destination. Four hour drive to the lodge, half of it on washed out dirt roads, and a little side delay to help some Cuban refugees. Soon we pulled into the compound that is Pesca Maya. All through the ride I was looking for hurricane damage. It had been just a short of two months since Dean slammed head on into this part of Mexico, yet we didn't see any no-ticeable catastrophic damage. But as we rolled up to the main lodge, we could see where the guest huts had roof and wall damage. The Lodge owner already had a crew on site working to put everything back together.

We had a splendid Mayan style room only 60 feet from the surf, washing in on a beautiful white sand beach. There was a path to the main lodge that wound through palm trees and gorgeous local plants and flowers of the region. The path was crowded with little lizards, large iguanas and sand crabs that would poke their heads out then disappear as you strolled by. The main lodge was exquisite, the food off the hook, but the most important resource in the Lodge was a young man named Juan whose job it was to survey the guests drink glasses, and just before they got to the last swallow, he would get them another soft drink, beer of cocktail.

One day when we came back from fishing, we learned that fresh lobster was on the menu along with fresh local fish. Lindsay was mingling with the Cooks and servers, and she noticed the head chef looked very tired. He explained in his very good but slightly broken English he had to free dive all morning to CATCH the fresh lobsters. We had 14 people at the Lodge this week, and it wasn't just one lobster per person.

First day out with Darian the head guide and a different Juan then the Drink Captain at the lodge, Juan the apprentice guide. Darian was very professional, smartly dressed, spoke very good English and was a pure gentlemen. Juan was a tad shy until it was time to get his angler casting to a fish. Then he was all business. I would be working with Juan, while Lindsay and Darian would be a team. This was our very first time ever fishing Salt water flats, and we had heard over and over to strip strike bone fish and not to lift the rod like northern trout anglers.

And of course on the first half dozen shots we both lifted our rods on the strike and missed the fish. Finally, we hopped out of the boat to wade a flats in search of fish. We moved along side by side about 100 feet apart. I said to Juan, "Lindsay will end up catching the first bone fish...you watch". My words were still hanging in the warm humid air, when Lind's and Darian quickly dropped to a crouch and Lind's got her fly airborne. A decent 40 foot cast...strip strip strip, and I see her strike correctly now her rods in the air and line melting off the reel into her backing for which through all the steelhead and salmon she had caught. Had never actually seen her backing. I smiled at Juan with my "Told You So" grin.

What a great week of fishing. On Wed. of that week I had a wonderful shot at a Grand Slam. After catching bone fish for two solid days and finally doing very well at it, Lind's and I decided we wanted to try Tarpon and Permit. We had to make about a 45 minute run in the Panga to get to a group of mangroves that held local Tarpon and a good number of Bones and Permit.

We are SCREAMING across an open flat.....when I hear Darian, and Juan starting to talk fast and excited in their native tongue. Which we got a kick out of all week, our guides talking in Spanish, and raise their voices to a crescendo level and then turn to us, and calmly say there is a Permit over there, or a crocodile, or shark. However, they didn't need to translate to us this time, they were yelling PERMITTA PERMITTA PERMITTA. I could see this fish, the flats were a tad muddy from the wind, yet this large dark creature stood out like a buffalo in a snow storm. Personally, I thought it was a Tarpon because it was huge. Turns out it was the largest Permit Darian who had been guiding at the lodge for over 10 years had ever seen with his sports. This fish was in the high 30's to possibly over 40 pounds. We got in front of where we thought the fish was moving, and hopped out of the boat, Juan and I trying to close ground on the fish and get a shot. But the big fish kept angling away from us. This wasn't a flat like we had been walking the first two days. It was soft mud, and trying to move quickly along it was difficult, or should I say difficult for me. Juan was in stellar shape and probably could have run the fish down and tailed it.

We decided the boat was our best chance to get a shot, so we hustled back and climbed in. Darian positioned us again and I hopped up on the bow. This monster is coming right at us...and I make a decent cast ..didn't spook him and he paid no attention to my Merkins crab. Blew the second cast, and the fish swam right to the boat made a swipe of his huge body alongside the boat splashing water into the cockpit and swam straight away. I made a desperation going away Hail Mary cast, and laid the crab a foot and a half in front of him and then it happened...being a novice, I determined the cast was a poor one, and began to pick it up and effectively pulled the crab right OUT of the Permits mouth as he lunged for it. Game Over

Darian was crushed. He was way to cool to yell or get mad. What

I realized is, the nature of these marvelous guides is the fact they take pride in guiding their sports to trophy fish to have the biggest of a species caught by their anglers. In this case Darian would have been the Permit King back at the lodge and in his village.

Into the Mangroves we went, I could tell Juan and Darian were a little down from my screw up on the permit so we searched the mangroves for cursing Tarpon. They are scanning hard, I look out into the open water right in front of me while they are sweeping the edges of the vegetation and I see a 40 pound class Tarpon sunning itself. I say there's one, as my line is immediately in the air. I land the fly three feet to the right of the fish, two strips BANG fish on. I get four jumps out of him, and he runs to the back of the boat to where I have to raise the rod to get over Darian who's up on the platform and the Tarpon comes off. Didn't see another Tarpon or Permit the rest of the day, and we finished up by catching some bigger bones.

On this trip Lind's was into kissing the bone fish before she let them go. She easily kissed 40 bones in a week. We get back from our "Almost" grand slam trip, and are in great spirits. What an exciting day. The cocktail hour was nothing short of festive talking to the other guests about our experiences with the slam opportunity. After dinner the cocktailing continued. Lindsay loves Margareta's. And you get the REAL deal in Mexico. We probably stayed a little longer then we should have and the walk back along the beach was wonderfully romantic. We fell into our comfortable bed, exhausted from an exciting day, absolutely a little drunk from all the fun.

At 4 AM and only having slept for about three hours I opened my eyes and was wide awake. I had been dreaming of a fly pattern. This wasn't unusual for me. Many times the night before a fishing outing I dream up a fly pattern and usually have to tie it before going fishing that next day. My dilemma however, was my lovely sweetheart can't sleep with any light in the room. If you are charging your cell phone, you have to lay it face down on the nightstand so there is perfect pitch black in the room. "Honey"....Honey? "What is it"? she reluctantly said. "Honey I have a fly pattern in my head, and I need to tie it before we head out today". We have to be out the door for breakfast at 6 AM...it's 4 AM......and I need to tie a few of these so I need to get started now". You can imagine Lindsay's reaction to this request. She wasn't buying into it. I offered to set her up out on our beautiful Veranda overlooking the Ocean in a lounge chair and she could have the pounding surf rock her back to sleep.

Now my girl is a huge sport. She is the kind of gal who is rugged when she has to be. I can tell you she has never said..."honey I have to pee...can we break down our rods and good find a rest room?" No not Lind's, she'll find a secluded spot and pee in the woods. On this trip if she had to pee during the day, she'd hop in the water and pee. So in her grogginess she grabbed pillows, a blanket and made a camp out on our deck.

I love studying the natural critters that fish eat and try and duplicate them into a fly. I had been watching these shrimp and small crabs we'd been seeing while walking the flats. There was a color scheme that stood out to me...size and shape. I knew I had the materials to tie what was in my head. I got to work with my vice and the bureau lamp and spun a half dozen of these flies.

About 5:30 Lind's came in from the deck as the breaking light came up over the surf to witness a gorgeous sun rise. We showered away some of the cocktail fog from the night before and got down to the main lodge for breakfast. Darian asked what we wanted to shoot for today. I said back to the Bones, and maybe some mangroves where we might find a Tarpon or big Snook. He knew just the place and it was only a 10-minute boat ride.

We eased up on a flats that we hadn't been on before. Luckily we were the first ones there. The game this day was for Lind's and Darian to walk the flat and fish for Bones. Juan and I would bone fish our way into the back of this expansive flat to a stand of mangroves, circle up the other side along shore and back to the boat. I gave Lindsay a few of my Dream fly's and Juan and I took off. I hadn't gone 20 yards and already landed two nice bone fish on a different pattern that had been working for me.

Juan and I worked our way back into the mangroves and he stopped suddenly. He pointed to the water along the roots of a stand of brush moving. He said "big Snook". I had been making very accurate casts all week long up under the mangroves, and I did on this occasion as well, but we couldn't get this fish to play. We spent an hour in there looking around to no avail. So we fished our way back to the boat. I caught another bone fish on the way back, but found the fish spookier on the return trip.

About 100 yards from the boat I saw Lindsay sitting up front in the boat taking it easy. As we got closer I saw her enjoying an ice cold Cerveza with the biggest shit eating grin on her face. Once again I turned to Juan and said.."Oh my God ...she killed the fish while we were gone". I yelled out "How many"...Lindsay couldn't help herself... "I kissed 10...and lost another 6". As she completed her tally Darian... jumped on board..."Mang...YOU TIE KEEELER FLY". Even when Lindsay make bad cast....all of a sudden I say strip strip he coming". I tell her 12 o'clock she land the fly at three, and still they come. We started laughing, and I looked at my dream fly. It had about two twists of materials left on it. Lindsay said she'd asked Darian if she should put on a fresh fly, one just like it and he'd say no. Fish still eat it.

Lindsay, The Flats Kissing Bandit....

Darian shared the fact that Lindsay had hooked so many fish, two other guides with their sports were somewhat embarrassed they couldn't get their men into fish and left the flat because they were tired of seeing her rod bent.

One last interesting note. On our last day we switched guides. I got to fish with Darian. We landed on the "Keeeler" fly flat, and I tied on the Dream Fly. I had shots at several fish, made good casts, pulled the fish right up to the fly and got one refusal after another until we knew it was time to change the fly.

Since that day, Lindsay has never debated my getting up and tying a fly I've dreamt about, however at home I can walk up into our fly tying office and she can sleep in the peace of our pitched dark bedroom.

Panga, the workhorse of the Flats

11

"Getting into the Swing of things"

FOR MAYBE THE first time all day I stuck the anchor point of my pick up, perfect D Loop and I knew as I forced the 14 foot two hander forward, I felt the power surge just perfect like hitting a baseball flat dead center, and 90 feet of line ran to the far bank and settled in. The band in my head started playing a familiar tune from Spielberg's 1975 Classic Jaws. Daaaa da...Daaaa da, the fly swept into the Apex and lighting struck and lit my right arm up as if it had burst into flame. The violent head shakes like the lion taking down the stag on the African plains. The surging forward of the upper half of my body as I bent to the pressure of a big fish rolling up to the surface to spit my offering back at me.

But the hook had found flesh and the fish knew he was in trouble not panicked, just that this encounter was more of a nuisance then expected. He burrowed downstream and then in a flash of light sped right at me. A 14 foot two handed rod and a heavy large arbor reel has not the same nimbleness of a three weight trout reel and a 12 inch fish, so I fumbled and stumbled to catch up to the fish...backing up...in the boulder strewn bottom....reeling and pulling in line at the same time...until I was tight to the fish once again. And now for the first time he was broad side of me flexing his muscles, like a boxer just before he hits the ring after working his body into a pre-fight sweat and tuning his every muscle for the 15 rounds ahead.

The violent heads shakes and if this big fish could scream at me his emotions would be unprintable. He switched gears and left the scene and took me back out into the big water, more rolls to the surface coupled with surges back and forth.

Long rod, heavy tippet but rather small stinger hook on the stern of my Waddington Shank fly creation, so I was careful not to punch myself out in the early rounds. Steelhead have steel heads, they just don't know how and when to give it up. "No quit" I could hear his corner man yelling to him "Stay off the ropes". But this time I was going to win and after a few tense moments the fish knew it too and eventually succumbed to the bend of the 14 footer and slid along-side my kneeling position near the bank. Husky fish, full of muscle, yet exhausted.....I eased the fly free, gently pointed him into the current for a drink of fresh air and he lumbered back into the emerald flow.

"PLAYA"

Throughout this sequence, the excitement that was the initial grab by the fish of my fly was overwhelming me so much that the catch and release were matter fact. It's a drug created by the "pull", that engulfs your brain and smolders for quite some time. For me even with pictures of these great animals to look at, remembering that moment revolves around the "Grab"…"Take" "Tug" "Pull" of the violence that is the killer instinct of a Big Trout or Salmon.

Swinging flies are most notably done with two handed rods, but heck swinging a fly is easily done, still is and has been for over two hundred years with single hand rods as well. Presenting the fly down stream and across in a fashion that suggests a wounded or disoriented bait fish becomes an opportunity for a Predator fish that lives to kill and eat them.

I'm somewhat of a traditionalist. As I take on a new hobby or sport I like to understand the roots of its existence. Fly fishing roots are of course from the womb of the British Isles. I enjoyed studying about those gentlemen. Traditions with Gilly's, proper etiquette, attire and fly fishing process. But there was another world of fly fishing going on in the British Isles that had spread to the Nordic region of Europe. Long fly rods, that men swung with double tapered lines to make 100 foot casts in their quest for the Crown Jewel of the Isles, the Atlantic Salmon. At the time I got interested in this, there was no Internet, Google or U-Tube to research this style of fly fishing.

One day in 1994 I walked into my local fly shop. In the rack was a G Loomis GL3 14 foot two hander. I was romantically swept off my feet at the site of this stick. I picked it up and took it outside to wiggle it. We have some big rivers in my region of Lake Ontario, and I envisioned in my mind that our stocked yet migrating steelhead and salmon would take to a swung fly just as they do in Europe, and the budding "Spey" fishery on the North West coast.

Without knowing anything remotely on how to cast this thing I decided to jump in. The shop owner acted as if he knew how to handle these rods and took me out on the lawn to show me and in fact he knew nothing of the sort. I had a reel that could handle a long belly double taper line, and the only reference material I could find on how to cast this stick was Hugh Falkus's book which they had at the fly shop thank God.

I spent many hours looking at the step by step pictures trying to emulate his casts. Taping up the Ferrules as he instructed, and going down to an outflow from a power plant that had room and a flow for me to swing this thing around until I was able to get the line out and present the fly.

Finally it was fall fishing time, and my buddy Gratson and I hit one of our favorite little streams. Now the term little is key, because this was way too much rod for a stream that was 60 feet wide at best. Heck the rod was a third the length of the width of this stream.

Didn't matter I wanted to catch a fish on this rod. In those days there wasn't nearly as much pressure on these tribs as there is today, and we didn't have anybody else around. Good thing because I looked very awkward trying to fit this long fly rod into this system. We came to this one nice run, the Island hole. It has some frothy water at the head of the island, that dumps into a nice long deep run at the tail. By now Gratson had watched me screw around with this thing for an hour and asked if he could try it. Sure...I handed him the rod, and he lobbed a cast out, swung the fly through the riffle to the tail, and KABOOM a big steelhead grabbed the fly and high tailed it down stream but luckily came unbuttoned. I say that because dam it, I WANT to catch the first fish on this rod.

A few minutes later I hooked and landed about a 2 pound brown trout to break the ice, but obviously he didn't put much of a bend in the rod. And so it started, and now two decades of spending most of my time on migratory fish with a two hander. Oh how this sport has evolved with space age rod tapers and materials, and the lines that are available now, make casting especially at startup so much easier. Add in the countless Video's available on line and the learning curve is much shorter then when I started.

Why the love of the two hander? There is a long list of good reasons why. No back casting, fishing tight spaces along tree lined and bramble banks, covering lots of water not available with single hand rods…..BUT the one thing that sits at the top of the list is this……THE TUG

In swinging a streamer down and across a run, a fly engineered to swim as natural as the real thing, if you do it right, make the proper presentation you unlock the holy grail of reaction from the fish. In that instance when you entice a fish to come to the fly, you are going to experience the most primal instinct that fish was born with…to KILL your fly with the ferociousness and speed that God provided it as an angry adult salmonid. The engulfing of your fly by a fish with that kind of power, attitude and intention will send an electronic impulse up the fly line, through the rod, into your arm and transport it to your brain, and the euphoria of that connection …the "TUG"….will reduce you to a blabbering idiot …..melt your face down, and in an instant be as powerful as any legal or illegal narcotic and turn you into a TUG ADDICT.

It's even more powerful if you get into a mesmerizing state of Zen, cast step, cast step, focusing on the casting mechanics, as it's plenty of moving parts. It's repetitious and one can lose site of the fact they have feathers and fur tied to a hook at the end of these beautiful casts. Then… sudden IMPACT jerks you back to reality and makes you shiver at the fact you weren't paying attention almost as if you just got T-Boned at an intersection. But didn't get a scratch on you.

It's pretty difficult to get past what many who fly fish would state as their holy grail the rise to the surface of a fish to eat a floating fly, but you can get the best of both worlds skating a fly on the swing and have a great fish come and kill it. Just as you've seen in these memories of mine, I love all styles of fly fishing, but getting a fish to play on the swing is the ultimate sport for me, and it's become popular throughout the US and Canada just as it did in Europe many years ago.

I've caught so many memorable fish, fishing the two handed rods, stories already told in the chapters that proceeded this text. The grabs and spectacular fights can become a blur, but one of my latest successful catches runs up the leader board of great fish using this method.

One April, I was alone fishing the famous Salmon River in New

York State. This location has about two miles of perfect "swing" water with several long pools, runs and glides connected by boulder strewn fast riffles and pocket water laced into each of these runs. Being later April the water temperature had poked it's head into the lower 40 degree range to where drop back steelhead and maybe a few fresh arrivals would easily locate themselves in any of these diverse holding lies.

As usual nothing is ever normal with the Spring weather in Western New York. One year it's in the 80's in late April, the next it's snowing. We had had some warm days prior to my arrival so snow melt off the Tug Hill area above the Salmon River falls and reservoir was in full force and the river was running at 1,500 CFS. This flow chases a lot of people away. Not easy to wade, and for the fly fisher who is trying to nymph fish this water, it becomes more of a challenge. For us Swingers, a Scandi or Skagit line, with a moderate sink tip of 10 to 15 foot will put our streamers in a zone over a four to five foot deep section of river down a foot or so, and if there is a "Player" around, entice them to come to the fly.

Much like fishing a dry fly which is my other love in fly fishing, you are bringing the fish to the fly. So on the swing, I hope to pull that fish from its holding spot to my fly with the same attitude as a ferocious middle linebacker like Butkus or Nitschke had in lining up a running back to DEVESTATE them with a bone crunching hit.

How often have you had this sense of urgency and nervous excitement when you arrive to your fishing destination? Not many people around, you know where you want to start, it's a popular spot, only three cars in the lot for 2 miles of river and will this spot you have in mind be vacant? The trail leading to the water from the parking lot is about a half mile with a decent climb down into the river course. The walk through the woods is supposed to be soothing, calming, fresh leaves on the tress others still budding. You might see a deer or a turkey, but that walk in is never calming. I'm not your (and shame on me in a sense) average nature guy who will stop to look at something on the way in. I have a mission, my mind is racing,

(1) am I satisfied with the fly I choose to start with, I expect the river to be clear even while high)…(2) at 1,500 CFS, I've laced on the 12 foot of type five inches per second sink tip, wonder if I should have started with the seven, (3) but then if that's too heavy, I'd hang up on my first or second cast and that is a lousy way to start the day, (4) man the wind is howling I have the 540 grain head on, did I pack the 600?

By this time I'm at the top of the stairs and below me I can hear the river flushing in a roar that is drowning out the wind. Still not intimidated by 1,500 CFS, since I fish 2,000 CFS routinely on my home river, but the Salmon River is narrower so the speed and hydraulics has to be dealt with.

At the top of the steps I can almost see the entire run I want to start in., I don't see anybody around including the tail out which happens to be the sweet spot. My heart jumps a little with excitement as if reading my lottery scratch off ticket and I have the first three numbers. The run is open and at this flow, so much more water presents itself as perfect lies for these hard fighting migratory fish.

Clouds are circling and gathering to start a storm and I break out the rain jacket. Sure enough only minutes in it starts to rain and blow harder, but my choices on the rig I was throwing were dead on. So while the conditions were nearing dreadful, I was in a zone, casting and covering each lie with precision. I had taken a number of fish from January right into April in this very run, and with each cast and step I fully expected to get the "TUG". I'd uncork a 90 foot laser, toss in a quick mend and then hang on tight for the enviable….but each cast invariably ended down stream on the hang, and I'd step and cast again.

Once through the run, twice through the run, new fly, and then a third. Nobody home, or nobody willing to play. The wind was like the surf on an ocean beach. It would gradually build, rushing to shore explode on the sand and gently wash away. The rain was simply spitting rather than down pouring. It was a nuisance, but not a distraction. We all love to get a fish early in the game. NOT on the first or second cast because that's usually the death sentence for the rest of the day. So I was OK not to turn a fish on the first pass, but coming up empty on pass number two and three left me a little forlorn. Tons of water to hit, so I moved on downstream.

At the tail of this property , it dumps into the estuary that leads to Lake Ontario. This area is very popular for incoming and outgoing fish. This time of year the lower section which is just classic two hander water is very popular and though there was only two other cars in the lot I fully expected those anglers could be just two, or two car full of people wandering around here some place. For as far as I could see, not another soul. So while I probably half-heartedly fished my way in that direction, my mind was racing once again on what system I'd fish once I got down there.

Approaching the Meadow is much like the Flats, can't see the entire run on the way in, only the top end, and you have to turn the corner to see the entire landscape. Nobody up top, but as I rounded the corner, there were three people fishing, one being a guide with his sports. I knew this guy, and we exchanged pleasantries. His sports were fishing spinning rods with flies and or egg sacks. Lou knew me, and my game well enough to split the water up between us, with me fishing and casting down away from his guys, plus giving them free rein to fish down with me.

There are many debates among anglers on fishing web message boards Spin VS Float VS Fly VS Spey or Two handed fishing all not getting along. I'm more than willing to share water with others, no matter what method of angling they aspire to, as long as they are doing it legally. Having been a guide for many years I will always defer to a working guide and his folks since he's working and I'm just playing.

So Lou and I had a game plan, his folks kept fishing and I got to fish some of my favorite water that was at a great flow, and fully expected to hook up. I grinded away down the Meadow, snapping off one long cast after another swinging the streamer directly downstream of me to the bank which was good holding water in its own right (you'll see that later) and nothing. Not a nip, or tick, or what is known in the two handed fishing circles as a "Pluck" from a fish.

Hmmmmm. What the hell is going on here? Checking the reports on the river web site, they had hit some nice fish here early this week. Maybe they all dumped out to the lake, and there is a lull in their migration. Now understand expectations of us swingers is not that we think we'll light up a large number of fish. For me, even one fish or a couple tugs puts me at even with the house, anything over that, I'm playing with the houses money. Looked at my watch. Made my first cast right at 7 AM. It was now 11:30. Four and a half hours and nary a sniff from a fish.

I round the bend and am back alone with my thoughts and the howling breeze from the lake, and successfully washing every streamer, shank intruder, and tube fly in my box and end up fishing right to the estuary. Now it's 12:30 PM. Time to decide what to do. I talk to myself all the time. I'll ask a question in my mind, and answer it verbally. "You paid your dues in fishing this prime water. You've covered over a mile and a half of it without a violent interruption from a fish. Had it been a pretty day, birds singing, eagles soaring overhead, I might have chalked it up as a nice walk while fishing expedition. I might very well have decided to unstring the two hander, head to town get a cold beer, a sandwich, and probably fish up river some place. I knew there were plenty of fish up river. I wanted the solitude of fishing the lower end. I had only been around a few people today, I knew them, it was pleasant, I might have even called it a day had I even pricked a fish.

But now it was getting personal. This is end of April, some 20,000 steelhead had run this river to drop their eggs. There is probably several 1000 still swimming around somewhere in these 11 miles to the Dam, and I can't find ONE? Started to make a slow walk back towards the Meadow, came around the point of an island mid river and the place is empty. Nobody there. No matter how tired, windblown, damp from the on and off showers, you simply can't walk past this place without trying it again. I get to the very top of the meadow, that includes a fast chute with a frothy topping on the rush of water tumbling into the long wide river bed. I've watched countless Pacific Salmon rip up through this rapid in the fall, and had many memorable days catching fish at the head of this spot as they staged to make that next burst up river.

There is a great rock to sit on at this place, hang your boots in the water, as you either contemplate the problems of the world, or in your own life, as well as the good things, and it's a great spot to re-rig. I'd been hammering away at this for six full hours without anything to show for my efforts. What to try next? The human silence I enjoyed was broken by some mumbling behind me. Hard to hear over the water rushing by and the wind, but I turned to see two more anglers had arrived. These guys were toting two handers as well, and the muffled mumbling was them asking if I was willing to rotate the run. I obliged and even offered them first shot at it, mainly because I decided to sling a 15 foot 7 IPS tip on with my number one go to Intruder fly. An off white fleshy colored articulated contraption I had come up with that had a dozen steelhead on its scorecard so far this past winter and spring.

One of the guys was another familiar face..."It's Craig right"? "Yeah" said Craig. We spent a couple minutes with me giving him my report with all the blanks in it for nothing is happening. Craig was insistent that I go first but again I declined as I needed a rest and re-rig. So Craig and the other guy start step casting the Meadow. A few minutes later as the space up top opened, I was rigged and ready. This very spot is another place where I've had recent success. The fast water is actually parted by a near shore stretch of a deeper slot and flatter water. I've caught some nice steelhead and brown trout in that flat water cuddled up next to the froth the past few months. The very first cast with the new polly leader and fly, and at the end of my swing I get a quick hard take but don't connect.

Interestingly, I wasn't dejected but rather encouraged on the miss that there was at least one player around. A sign of life, and I wasn't even to the sweet holding spot yet. It was four or five steps down stream. Maybe it was a random drive by hit, or maybe the 15 foot of 7 IPS was putting me in a zone I was either over or under all day. Four casts later there I am. Lined up just above the holding water that has given up some great fish. After six full hours of fishing I had the hydraulics figured out, and knew where to land the fly to get the proper speed on the presentation through this holding spot. I have to mention that for the last few minutes the wind had died down, and the "SUN" was trying to squeeze past the crowded clouds above.

Now all along I've described the "TUG" as the medicine that makes a swinger an addict. I made an adequate cast, but what happened next is a fish boiled, ate the fly and pushed a wall of water and white spray to the surface shaking her head violently before I felt the power in her take. That was short lived by a few milliseconds because after hooking herself, she rocketed out of the water in three long grey hound jumps bending my 13 footer towards the water and making my chatty reel scream like a rabbit in a wolf's jaw. My Peerless makes enough noise that anybody within the same zip code can hear it, and immediately Craig and his friend who were 30 yards down river jerked around in surprise as if an ambulance was screaming down behind them. Now this big fish who I've seen completely naked while suspended in the air was fast into my backing and roaring past my angler friends. I had scooted out of the water up onto the bank and was at a full dead run reeling as fast as I could to get even or below this beast of a fish. For some reason Craig looked dumbfounded as I asked to move past him, while he stood frozen in the water.

I navigated around Craig and settled in to regain my authority and bring the fight to the fish. One thing I noticed, is this fish was full bodied, not long and lean like a drop back fish. She made three more blistering runs and several more leaps and surface thrashing head-shakes before I could lead her to the shallows and unhook her. Easily mid teens pounds wise of sterling silver hen. A full egg wagon who either hadn't received the invite to the spawning party or because she was true royalty, decided to show up fashionably late. Successfully released, she sped away back into the river in a manner that suggested she had an attitude about her on the fact that I had interrupted her plans of migration that day and made her late.

Craig was unnoticed until now, but he was nearby admiring the fish. Once again he offered to let me go ahead, but I insisted that since I had caught a fish, I was comfortable in relegating myself to third rod position behind him and his partner. They fished their way down, and I behind them. I had another quick tug up top and a quick on and off of a fish, and now three quarters down with Craig ahead of me, I swung the fly right into shore where I knew the river bed is rutted with a three foot deep trench. On the hang down I'll pull my rod arm back then slide the fly downstream again while holding the rod at my side. It's become as normal a routine as a musky angler "figure eighting" his bait at the end of their cast before re-casting. As I slid the fly back, I got the telltale hard tug we all fish for, and almost at Craig's boot tops an 8 pound Steelhead is airborne causing Craig to jump back to the bank. This was a true drop back and while she was angry and put off by the sting in her jaw, she didn't have the pugilistic tendencies her fresh sister had earlier.

Fish was landed, gently released, and I wandered back up top. It was now 3 PM. And while the gates to the ranch didn't close until 6 or 7 PM I had decided not to overstay my welcome, and bid my fisher friends a good day.

The Sun had come and gone and the wind returned. The walk out is a pretty one, yet even in breathable waders, the march up a steep hill along a corn field bordering the river brings you out of your great day trance. The rest of the stroll through the woods is pleasant, I noticed some wild flowers, I did see both an Eagle, and an Osprey soaring overhead, and even some gnarly old tree trunks that may have been around since the revolution for all I know.

Funny how I can refocus on my surroundings after getting the job done.

12

Small Streams and Trickles

I AM REMINDED each time we pull up on a dirt road in the mountains of Pennsylvania by my friend Joe, of the first time he brought me here and I spied the stream we were about to fish, that I realized I could "Jump" over. I asked if there was a lake or pond at the top of this hill we were going to fish. Nearly 20 years later I am silently reminded what a stupid fucking question THAT was.

Up to that point in my resurgence back into fly fishing some 25 years ago, I had been fishing large to moderate flows. I worked with Joe, and he kept showing me pictures of these beautiful wild brook trout, and brown trout he was catching in PA up in the mountains. While I was fishing bigger flows and for bigger fish the one character trait I don't have to get over or adjust to was "big' fish syndrome. I'm happy catching cookie cutter blue gills off our dock with a 3 or 4 weight, getting that same rush on every fish for it eating my fly or popper from the surface as I can be fishing for Steelhead and Salmon. So one hurdle I had already jumped was my eagerness to chase these little 6 to 12 inch Brookies.

The Gemstone of the Pennsylvania Mountain streams

Joe, his brother, his dad and his friend Ron and I made many trips to the mountains. The other guys had and have traditionally fished these small trickles with an ultra-light rod and garden hackle. And man they know how to read water and find holding fish. Joe also tossed tiny spinners which I found fascinating. Many times Joe and I would leap frog each other up the mountain streams. When he was tossing that Panther Martin, I'd often stand behind him and watch. It amazed me back then, looking into a tiny run or hole without spotting any fish, as soon as that blade started spinning through the slot a decent size Brookie or Brown trout would come out of nowhere and slam his lure.

I think I'm partially responsible for Joe taking up fly fishing. I was never going to catch as many fish as my worm dunker partners as I affectionately named them, but I'm not a big numbers guy. I'd rather catch them with a fly and when Joe started to see these fish raise to the surface and gobble a tiny dry fly, he started showing up with a fly rod along with his trusty spinning gear.

We had a wonderful rhythm on these trips. We stay at some marvelous Bed and Breakfasts along one of the main creeks in the North Central region called Kettle Creek. One place was right on the creek, so with breakfast being 8 AM, we'd get up and fish for two hours before breakfast. Next, eat and sit around for a bit to digest, then each day we made plans to hit one of the 100's of freestone streams rolling down the Sproul and Susquhanic State Forests mountains. All up dirt roads, with different levels of difficulty. The difficulty mostly being on the Fly fisher who had to deal with the forest cover in making accurate casts. We'd fish till midafternoon, come back to the B&B either make our own dinner, or grab something at the local Gin Mill, and then be back on the water from say 7 PM till dark fishing the night hatch. The streams in this region are Fort Knox rich with aquatic life

Those first few years I was toting around a 9 ft four weight, which was wonderful for the evening hatch fishing in wide open Kettle creek, but rather troublesome up in the mountains. In fact on my very first trip I broke the tip off my 9 footer, but fished it any way. Over the years I've armed myself with six and seven foot rods, all nice slow Cane models that make the fishing as pleasurable as any fishing I do.

I often get into these debates with myself when I'm in these wonderful places. Like...if I had to I could just stay here and do this for ever. Just fish for these beautiful fish in this unimaginable surrounding beauty. However the other side of my brain jumps in and says.... two handers swinging to chrome steelhead and salmon, Tarpon, Bone fish, Stripe Bass, Fat Albert......in other words....embrace that age old Anthem by CSNY..."Love the One Your With".

I've been fortunate to be in the middle of a few Green Drake full bore hatches, to witness what everybody talks about. A bug that makes fish stupid. Several years ago, we fished behind the B&B in the morning caught a few fish, me getting them on dry's and some nymph's not a lot of activity. We had heard the Green Drakes were just starting that week, and this one night on the way back from dinner, I had a few of these B-52 size flies crash against my windshield. Joe and I looked at each other it's going to happen tonight. And sure enough it did, right about 8:30 PM the sky and surface of the stream was a snow storm of huge flies, but what was the most amazing, this very same spot I fished in the morning with little sign of trout had noses poking up in every inch of flow in front of me. Big fish, little fish, Brook trout, Brown trout, Ding Ding Ding, the dinner bell chimed and the entire trout community was at the town square to engulf these protein rich bugs. What a sight.

I had missed a few yearly trips with Joe and the boys for various reasons, and now I had my prodigy wife by my side on most fly fishing excursions. I wanted to introduce her to this type of fishing. She was becoming a very accomplished fly caster, and I felt she was ready for this challenge. Lind's is 100% like me, she's interested in any fish on a fly no matter if it six inches or six pounds. Plus she loves beautiful fish. Interestingly she had already delved into the Char family on a few of our trips to Alaska fishing for Dolly Varden and Artic Char. But had never caught and Eastern US Brook trout.

She had a nice little fly rod in the 7 foot range that would allow her easier casting in the forest, but this was going to be creeping around on her hands and knees and making pin point casts into a slot that was a foot or two target to catch a fish. **(Remember To make sure she can hear the BIRDS SINGING)**

First time in the deep woods with a fly rod, tiny little trickles and that first trip she got into the trees plenty. Or too close to the bank trying to catch a near shore seam and snag up. Told her when that happens call it done, go get your fly and we'll revisit this pool later. Over the years I had done much better at not being the broken record, simply because she was fully proficient on the water, and didn't need my help. But this was new, and on that first day I must have repeated myself on lining up a cast...ONE TOO MANY Times...and here it came... DAVE I CAN"T HEAR THE BIRDS SINGING!!!!!!!.

Lind's right off the bat was killer on the night hatches. First night she lands something like 10 or 15 fish on dry flies, picking them out of every seam, riffle and run where we were fishing. Maybe I only caught a few because I spent most of my time gently netting these beautiful creatures and taking pictures of Kettle Creek's new fly fishing Princess.

Recently, we hit Joe's favorite mountain stream. Full of wild Brookies, and this is a dark forest, so the fish are deep dark purples and oranges, yellows, and white. The colors are off the chain. I'm fly fishing with Lindsay, and Lindsay is taking a Brook Trout on a Dry fly on every cast in places that I had passed by as not being an ideal holding lie. She's machine gunning the fish left and right out of this pocket and that, I mean places that are six inches wide. She is as stealthy and as accurate as a Navy Seal as she moves from one spot to another. Over my shoulder I see a camera flash so many times, I have to check what little sky I can see through the canopy to confirm there isn't a lighting storm coming our way.

This past spring, I was on my favorite trib in North Central PA fishing a classic run between two shallow fast water sections. It was 25 inches in depth along a bank that had grass, and some downed saplings lining the edge constructed two perfect holding slots. Gently landed a size 16 Olive in the deeper run, and promptly hooked and landed a Brookie. Then tossed the fly along the far bank, and a nice Brookie in the 12 inch range streamed up after the fly and at the last second swirled away on a refusal. Sent the Olive back in again, last second said no thanks, and twisted away. On each cast of this pool I had picked the fly before letting it ride to the tail out which was pretty much featureless.

Decided to rest the fish, the run, and tie on another fly. This time an Adam's size 14. Lined up my approach, and on the very fish cast my pretty Brookie committed and I gently set the hook....the fish scurried around the run for a split second, and popped the fly. Nice fish in the 12 to 13 inch range, nice for fish in a run that was two foot deep, and 10 foot wide. Knowing I had pricked that fish, I realized act two of this drama was over. Decided to toss a cast down the middle and promptly caught another smaller Brookie.

I've always wondered how short a fishes short term memory is.

I've caught the same steelhead on the same fly on consecutive casts, so there was a possibility the nicer fish had lost track of time and the sting in its jaw and might be ready again. Down went my fly, but nobody home. For whatever reason I let the fly float all the way to the tail, and to my surprise a huge by this streams standards Brook trout takes a swipe at the fly and either misses or refuses....I was so dumbfounded that what had to be close to an 18 inch fish was sitting in this water at the tail is maybe 12 inches of water. Next cast clearly a refusal, but got an even better look at the fish. Passed over this spot for the half hour I was kneeling down in there simply because I didn't recognize it had potential.

In the end both of the bigger fish won out for this day. And I salute them as I often do when a fish has out smarted me or wiggled free of a hook up. That's what keeps us coming back time after time. I will visit that run again next year, highly doubt those two "Beasts" will still be in there, however, I know I won't overlook the tail of this run ever again.

Small Streams with Giant fish

When I describe small streams, it also includes small streams to the Great Lakes tributaries. For Lake Ontario every trickle and small stream will induce a run of migratory fish, King and Coho Salmon, Steelhead and Brown trout.

Recently Lindsay and I were fishing such a stream off Lake Ontario. It has a historic migration of lake run Brown trout. Yes in most places this stream maxes out at maybe 50 feet wide, and in many places even narrower. This day, we wandered into a run that has a sharp bend to the right forming a deep pool and tail out against several fallen trees and brush. First target is the deep run and we took turns fishing it to no avail.

One of the fallen tress created an arch with a little pool running off the main flow. This opening was no more than six feet wide. For kicks I tossed my streamer in there and stripped it out to not get hung up on the log, and got a sharp grab. Hmmmmm.... Somebody home in there. Two casts later I was tight to a five pound Brown trout. We chuckled at me digging out this player from his den. Lindsay shrugged her shoulders and stepped in the run, and made a perfect cast through the archway. Repeated it a couple more times and she came tight to an even bigger fish nearly 10 pounds.

Big fish can live in small places

Wow, two beautiful big lake run fish, holding in a spot smaller than a fifth grader. Can't happen again right? Five fish later , we looked at each other and decided to not overstay our welcome and walked off. So picking fish ...big fish out of cover on inland streams or rivers and trickles off the Great Lakes is a game all its own. The interesting thing about small streams is they are everywhere. Many of us don't realize just how many are nearby. Get a topo map of your state or region, goggle research it, or even go to the public library and look this up. Find the blue lines and make plans to visit them. You can do research to find out if they are stocked or if there are reported wild fish, or you can be an explorer and find out for yourself first hand.

13

A Day To Remember For Ever

IT WAS JUST getting light as I witnessed creases in the sky of the sun's first glimmer rays penetrating the dark background of the fading night. I stepped into the river. It was Sept 13 2002, it was going to be a warm day, sunny, and mild. Not classic Pacific Salmon fishing weather by any means, but this was my first trip of the season for fall run fish. The first few steps into the froth are baby steps to make sure you remember how to keep your balance. I crossed the river to the other side where there is a glide about 40 yards long. A small holding spot for migrating fish. There was already an angler there peering into the water. Not fishing, just standing erect and staring into the run. If he was standing on one leg I would have mistaken him for a Heron. I figured he was watching some fish. I eased up near him and asked his permission to fish the head of the run since he wasn't fishing yet. He said go ahead.

I know this place pretty well. Though it's small it has some interesting current breaks and pocket water. You have some flat water that mingles with some choppy water creating distinct seams at the head, middle and tail out and on a good day holding fish in all locations. I had a leach pattern tied onto the business end, and since I was swinging a 13 foot spey rod that morning, I was well off the rim of this run. My silent companion was several steps closer, but still not fishing. I uncorked a 40 foot cast, and swung the leach through the seam. I got a shoulder rattling jolt and was fast to a fish on the first cast. While it's great to get the first fish out of the way, I'm always leery of days that start out like this. Not being pessimistic, just in my experience you seem to fish very hard for the second bite of the day when the first one comes on the very first cast. Well this was a very hot silver king and he won the battle and escaped after a couple minutes. The very next cast I'm into another fish, land that one, and follow with the daily triple on the third cast. Finally my friend speaks up, man I don't see any of these fish you are hooking. With a halfcocked smile I told my new friend who graciously allowed me to step in and fish, to forget trying to spy them, just fish the water, read it and fish it.

As dynamic as the lake fishery is, the fall, winter and spring fishing on the Great Lakes tribs is not only dynamic, but at times traumatic and romantic. The quest for world class fish like the Steelhead, a migratory rainbow trout is pursued by anglers all over the world. Fall migrations of King, Coho, and Steelhead as well as big Brown trout keep the great lakes regions alive 12 months a year.

Since my new friend was gracious about letting me fish above him, I invited him to take my spot and fish this swing which was obviously holding a number of fish. This slot is a resting zone between two very hard white water runs where this kings sometimes with their backs out of the water sledge hammer through to get to a holding or resting spot, gobble up some needed oxygen, and then continue on their way. He thanked me and stepped in. Meanwhile I leap frogged down from him giving him plenty of room.

I found myself day dreaming for a minute that with so many salmon in this run, if a steelhead was anywhere near this zip code they might take the opportunity as they often do in the Salmon River, to set up behind these fish just in case the mother lode of nutrient rich salmon eggs started pouring down to them. With already having hooked three fish in the first 45 minutes, that would usually make any swinging anglers day, I said to myself, what the heck and uncased a Spey style fly to run down the seam in hopes that a player was there. On cast number three I got the solid take of a fish that came hard to the fly, but immediately knew this wasn't a king salmon as it rocketed in the air. The light was still coming up on the day, and I couldn't tell if this was a trout or possibly a dime bright Coho Salmon that ran in with the Kings. This fish took off downstream with me scrambling over the ragged bottom in hot pursuit. The fish ran up a braid to the main stem, and I was able to turn it and confirm my day dreaming had paid off. I in fact was looking at a steelhead in the 10 to 12 pound range with that sexy purple spey fly in its yap. The marabou flowing over its gums as the fish frantically swam in circles.

Then this fish did something no other fish had ever done to me before or since. Near the bank was a Muskrat or beaver hole, that likely went beneath the river bottom into the bank. The fish dove into that hole head first. It's tail wagging out of the hole. I reached down to grab its tail and it somehow exploded out of the hole and broke the shank of the fly and was gone. Dangling in my hand was a half-eaten Spey fly. I sat on a rock for a few moments and laughed to myself at what a crazy series of events had happened in the first hour of the new season. I had no idea what was going to happen next but I figured it might be epic....and it was.

My new friend hadn't hooked a fish yet, and was back to peering into the water. I could see the frustration on his face, but it was apparent that no matter how many fish I had hooked or would hook in front of him, his propensity for successful fishing could only include spotting them first. I'm sure when the light came up above the water, he'd have his shots. I bid him farewell, and walked down stream.

Understand, there wasn't five other people in sight for as far as I could see up and down river. So I had my choice of any slots to fish. I have another favorite holding spot rest area in the middle of the mayhem of frothy water, and stumbled my way back across the river as I was still getting my wading legs. This slot is a deep rut up along a bank lined by overhanging Willows. It made an S curve to the left and dropped into a plunge pool that emptied down to the fast water. The ultimate swing is to land your fly in the run against the bank and have it end down in the pool.

Once again, my first three or four cast were met with hard pulls and big bright Kings coming to the surface shaking their heads in violent windshield wiper style, and throwing the iron. WOW...how many fish can be in this run. I finally kept a 25 pound buck pinned and landed him in some slack water across the river. At this point the light was wrong for me to peer into this run. I had to cross over, get on that bank to see what was going on. I was so curious, I didn't care if I spooked the fish, I had never seen so many aggressive King Salmon come to a swung fly, on a floating line, with only the weight of the fly. My fly could only be 6 to 12 inches below the surface.

I went up river to cross so not to spook the fish, and get a vantage point behind a huge bolder on shore and hopefully not put these fish down. What I discovered was spectacular. There had to be thirty 20 pound plus fish in this run to the plunge pool. They were all fired up snapping at each other, and swirling around. Then a half dozen would jump out of the pool, and head up river while another half dozen poured in from the river below. It was rush hour in this run, and the tempers were flaring from these fish. And I decided to take ultimate advantage of that situation.

When trout and salmon are snapping at each other and rolling into each other they are pure suckers for anything to intrude their space. This is "Their" ritual. And no outsiders are welcome. I've seen a 25 pound King take an 8 pound Brown trout into its mouth sideways to remove them from the river dance. If I had a movie crew with me, I could have showed the world that unpressured King Salmon when in an aggressive mood will just about take a fly from the surface if placed in their den of spawning sin. I selected a sparse tie from my box, tied it on and now made the cast from the shore. I landed the fly so that when it reached the head of the pool the current would pull it to the surface. I watched fish after fish chase that fly into the surface film and hammer it. I'm truly not a numbers guy but I decided for the sake of science and research I'd keep score.

By 1 PM 27 salmon had attacked my fly and 1 steelhead. More than 20 fish had been hooked or pricked. The only reason I believe that many came to play is I had fresh fish tumbling into the run all the time. I only landed five or so more fish. They were big dime bright and a huge chore to handle once hooked because they were so fresh and powerful. The water was cool enough for them to fight hard and not be over stressed. By 1 Pm I was exhausted. I think the day time temperature was in the mid 60's but I was wringing wet with sweat, and I could no longer raise my arms above my head. I've had a few other opportunities to hook a lot of Salmon on special days similar to this one, and have cut the fishing short remembering the beating I took from those fish. At my age, I'm sure I'll never have a day like that again, because I won't allow myself to get in the ring and go toe to toe with that many powerful fish in one day.

An Epic day. I found out there were only 12 anglers fishing the Douglaston Salmon run that day. The estimate is that some 10,000 salmon ran into the river on Sept 13 2002. And I was one of the lucky dozen.

14

Was Hot, but Now..... I'm Not

FISHING THROUGH A bite slump, like a hitter who seems to hit everything right at the defense, or a 2 guard whose shot all of a sudden just isn't falling. I don't only swing flies at trout and salmon, but it's one of my favorite ways to fish. Right off the bat you are paring down the number of opportunities to get bit simply because you are fishing to a lower percentage of fish that will choose to come smack your fly. Fishing a nymph or indicator rig you are bringing the plate of goodies right to the fish's seat at the stream bed table. Swinging a streamer fly, is finding that one player at the table who will jump up and serve themselves.

Knowing the odds are in the houses favor with this kind of fishing doesn't mean you are settling for a 1 fish or 1 bite day. I've more often than not, as long as I'm fishing to pods of fish are going to get bit a few times during an outing. But it's not just the attitude of the fish, it starts with your presentation. Can't fault the fish if your casting and presentation is sloppy. So you continue to tinker and adjust, fly speed , depth the fly is swinging by adding or subtracting sink tip density or added weight or weight of the fly. Next might be where you land your cast. Little further upstream or downstream to get sink rate into play so the fly is at different location swinging through the "Sweet Spot" where you think the fish are holding.

You make all these adjustments hoping that after several casts from the last adjustment, this next step will put you in the strike zone, yet unless you've spotted some fish, you aren't even sure you are actually fishing to fish. It's entirely possible that your pretty fly has swung through at good speeds and different depths to nothing but rocks and boulders and some aquatic insects.

We have a world class river near my home. Gets a big run of King Salmon and Steelhead. We concentrate mostly on the Steelhead. This river has tricky under currents, flow speeds, and trenches that depending on flow height can be as deep as 10 feet. Adjacent to the trenches are gravel flats that the fish come up on to feed and mill around. Sometimes you'll get a fish to come up out of the deep water and take the fly, other times you'll only get a hard take up on the gravel. It's a river that takes concentration on your adjustments. You start to put together repeatable programs such as in this CFS flow, if I run these sink rate tips and this size and weight type fly, I've had good success, and there you have a place to start.

You know fish are around, cause the guys up or down stream from you have landed some. And you run your program, and tweak and adjust, and rest the run, and change flies, and so on.....and every cast is met with the same silence from the deep. I had a stretch on this river, where I caught fish in November, and didn't get another BITE and fish until the following March. Not that I didn't catch fish in other places, but on this river, which is my home court, my supposed to be home field advantage.....NO LOVE. Probably fished it seven or eight times in that stretch and couldn't get a pull. Meanwhile my buddies would text me, got a couple, missed a couple, everybody else seemed to be finding the strike zone but me. Like the hitter and the shooter, you just have to keep swinging, and keep shooting.

On that fateful March day, the river was a vision, deep green water surrounded by a white cape of fresh snow. Almost like one of those paint by numbers pictures. Stay in the lines the water was green and the banks and forest hugging the edges of this beautiful flow were white with a bit of green splashed in from the ferns along the shore. A light snow was falling at first, and then the skies cleared overhead and the brilliance was magnified when the Sun lit up the river and white powder.

Lindsay was below me, she hadn't caught a fish this day either, but she wasn't in a slump on this river. It's hard not to let yourself lower your expectations after so many fruitless encounters with the fish in this watershed. I remember I was at a point of confidence that the setup I was swinging was good enough to get bit. Fly, sink rate speed of the fly. It's March the water is still in the 30's, I don't expect the same physical mind jolting tug that one would get from a steelhead in warmer water conditions. I had fallen into the rhythmic cast swing step trance we can all fall into. It had been so long, like some hermit living up in the forest and it's been forever since he spoke his native language to another human. In a slump you talk to yourself a lot, you talk to the river, the Gods, the birds, and even the bugs....just what the FUCK is it going to take to get a pull out of a fish around here.

I was mid-way down the run....and it finally happened, and it was much more than a wakeup call pull. It ended up being one of those coming at full speed to eat the fly and run back to my safe house tug. Fish was way into my shooting line before he slowed down. He didn't do any air tricks cause the water was 34 degrees but he did show himself in head shaking tirades along the surface. The next thing that happened to me was.....UH Oh......don't screw this up, big fish lots of leverage, it's been so long since I fought a fish in this river I might have been a bit hesitant at first. I could feel the tippet rubbing across his teeth but then recovered in time to gain control and landed a husky Steelhead with my articulated leach attached to his tongue.

"FINALLY"

I was relieved, Lindsay was happy for me, she knew of my frustration. By now my shoulders were warm from the overhead sun beating directly down on us. There was no wind, and you could hear the river meandering along over the rocks. Not a rushing powerful sound like it can be, but as if it were at peace, and delivering a pat on the back, nicely done. I walked to the bank, broke down my rod, sat down in a comfy snow drift up against a log, tilted my head back to invite the warmth of the Sun, I was nearly at water level, so I could hear the gurgling while John and Lindsay continued to fish. I on the other hand was quitting on a high note. Yet also offering reverence to the fish Gods, and this river that I was not a gluten. I appreciated and gave thanks for that fish.

I finally got a pitch to hit and jacked it.

15

Karma

MY WIFE LINDSAY was on the board of the Catskill Fly Fishing Museum (CFFM). I'm but a member as after nearly 35 years of being president of this club and that organization I no longer thirsted for a power position in either a professional guide's association, fishing club or national organization. I'm happy to help out with events and volunteer for things but I was taking a break from running, managing, or organizing anything.

Each year the CFFM inducts Fly Fishing Icons into their Hall of Fame. The Catskills are often recognized as the birthplace of American Fly Fishing, and the most iconic names of all time adorn the museum walls. From Theodore Gordon, Lefty Kray, the Wulff's Joan and Lee, to the artists, authors and fly tiers that are forever famous in fly fishing. In 2015, One of the inductees happened to be my all-time favorite author John Gierach. I've read just about every word John has ever written in books and magazines. Why? Because I simply love his style. I love that his stories aren't full of fluff, but rather he tells it like it is, describes his thoughts about "what if", and or "why doesn't" something work out or end the way his logical (at least logical to him) mind thinks about being a fly fisherman.

He is "True" to his personification. He left his home state of Ohio after college in a time that people were getting out of college, and hitch hiking or driving an ol' second hand car across the country in search of adventure. Or they told themselves that, maybe to find themselves (seems deeper than John's reason...) or just to say "F" it, and go have fun cause they didn't have anything better to do. Lindsay got off the phone and looked at me. "Dave that was Jim at the museum" they need a guy to drive Gierach around for a few hours before the induction ceremony, and I volunteered you since I know you love his work so much".

HUH? Was my first expression. Now one might think that a guy who loves John's work so much would be simply thrilled to do this. I had actually met John at a Fly Fishing show back in Jan, shook hands, of course told him I loved his work, posed for a picture that was actually kind of cool. I didn't look like the gushing adoring Fan, and he didn't look like the Author ICON that he is. Just looked like two guys holding a cup of coffee, and saying hey!

Now I never considered any response but "Sure" But only having met John for the time it takes to say "love your work...say Cheese for the camera" I did come away with the perception that John was exactly as I had imagined him. A low key, easy going don't take yourself serious kind of guy. And what I had to get ramped up for is to not be some drooling, bombastic fool that wanted to ask him how he put together his pieces and books, and what was his favorite fly, or stretch of water to fish.

It was the first weekend in October and John was staying at the Dette's Fly Shop home of world famous fly tier Mary Dette and her even more famous parents (Walt and Winnie). I was to saunter in after he had breakfast with Joe Fox, (Mary's grandson and now the proprietor of this Iconic Fly Shop Holy Ground) , and ask John if he wanted to take a ride and look at some rivers. We didn't have time to fish, and John was only in town for a day and a half, so he just wanted to drive around in the mountains to kill some time. He didn't want to visit the fly shops in Roscoe because they knew he was in town, and he would have been besieged for book signings and such. John just wanted to be incognito. Dressed in his famous fishing hat, pair of jeans and old fishing shirt we jumped in my truck and took him on a tour of some of the local famous rivers.

One place he wanted to see live was the Covered Bridge over the Beaver Kill River made famous in dozens maybe 100's of paintings and photo's. Where Lee Wulff, among a host of epic Catskill anglers has stood in that very spot waving a stick. We pulled in and sat on an old log rail along the river and watched it meander by. There was nobody around on this fine October day. We didn't talk about John's books other than asking him about his next publication due out in 2017. We talked about fishing. Not technical fishing, but what we liked and even what we disliked about our sport in the millennium.

John's about 7 years older then I. But I offered that I've become an angler of reverence. I no longer need to catch a number of fish, or the biggest fish. I do go fishing to have some success, but these days I'm as interested in after having some success whether limited or highly so, I am able to sit along the bank and appreciate all that comes with the package. The wild life, the habitat and environment, being at peace with my surroundings. To simply breathe in and be thankful for the day. I use the term and I've heard others state this as well...to "Not Overstay My Welcome". I am sincere about this , and I've fished this way for many years now.

John I could tell felt me. He knew I wasn't just speaking the words, that from all John's work, I knew he was in the same place, and probably why more now than ever I got him. But now I think or hoped he got me as well. One thing John and I have in common is we've studied and researched philosophy. Not so much the science, but rather the reality of one's life that then fosters their philosophies of who they are, and where in the scheme of life they kind of fit into.

Our professional lives are on opposite ends of the spectrum. He's been a laid back as he describes himself fishing bum, who still took care of business no matter what to get by and be able to do the things he loves. In that we are similar, but my taking care of business is truly that. In the fast paced world of Corporate America. However, when it comes time to string a fly rod (especially a Cane rod which I have the same affection for as John) we could come together and probably fish together and maybe enjoy each other's company. The one thing I wasn't as aware of was John's belief in KARMA. I'm a huge believer in good and bad Karma. So seems is John, and we each exchanged stories of instances in our lives where we believe Karma came into play.

We ended our morning with a quiet lunch in a family Bistro on main street Roscoe that consists of a half dozen buildings. I spend much of my time fishing two handed rods for migratory Trout and Salmon, and through our conversations John told me one of the fish he enjoyed the most to chase with the long rods were Chinook Salmon in Alaska. John kidded that for my gracious company to him, I'd probably enjoy some good Karma soon. I dropped him off to get "dappered" up for his induction , then picked John up an hour later and drove him to the event. An enjoyable afternoon and evening. Shook John's hand at the end of the night and thanked him for a delightful day. I think he was pleased as well.

Next morning Lindsay and I packed up to leave the Catskills. We had fished an evening hatch of fall Olives two nights before and contemplated on trying some fishing on the Beaver Kill before we left, but our primary plan was for a detour out of the Catskills to the Salmon River near Pulaski in search of the migrating King Salmon ascending that watershed. The salmon migration up to the first of October could best be described as a "dud". Fish were showing in trickles. But since we are season pass holders at the private Douglaston Salmon Run (DSR) property just up from the estuary we figured we'd see if any fresh fish were slipping in.

It was a beautiful sunny mild late morning when we arrived. Not typically a good King Salmon migration weather pattern. But we rigged up our two handers and strolled down the stairs to the river's edge. We both had fished for the Kings earlier in Sept. each having a take or two but not landing any of the players. King Salmon are not a very accommodating bity fish on a swung fly as they enter spawning tribs. They truly are on a mission to procreate and fishing our method of a tight line downstream swing isn't as effective as other techniques.

However for Lindsay and I the take of a swung fly with a fish the size of our Great Lakes Kings and their ornery attitude is what gets it done for us.

As usual we started about mid-way down this nearly 3 mile stretch of water, and fished some of our favorite places. We had plenty of room on this lazy Sunday afternoon. We were encouraged as several fish showed themselves working their way up the river towards the upper end of the best spawning grounds. We fished runs and pockets with no results, even some side channels that took a little more maneuvering with the longer rods where we had spied a few resting fish. Took a water and snack break and decided to move down to our favorite swinging run in hopes that some late day fish would break out of the estuary and come storming up.

Lind's started at the top of the run, while I moved half way below to start our step cast routine. Now, many have success fishing big bright gaudy flies for Kings, and I had run some of those patterns, but we were dealing with a lower flow, and gin clear conditions. I opened up my sparsely tied selection box, and spied a fly my wife designed and made famous in one afternoon hooking six huge steelhead on it, on the swing. It was a fly she tied in honor of a Lady Solider, LT Col. Tissa Strouse as Tissa was heading back to War in Afghanistan. Dark black, purple and blue dressed Spey style fly, with some red and blue trim.

I tightened down the Uni knot, stripped out enough line to cover the arc of the swing from across to downstream of my position, and cut loose a covering cast. Now in the back of my mind I heard the echo of Gierach's voice on obtaining good Karma for my good deeds from the day before. I had seen a few fish swirling around below me. So I knew there were fish in an about the tail of this run. About the fourth cast I was jolted with the hard pull of a fish and before I could even raise the rod, the fish was into 100 feet of backing. I have to admit after probably three hours of fishing without a tug, I was in a bit of a trance. NOW... lighting had struck and my haze was cleared and I immediately stepped down river rolled the rod to the downstream side and applied enough side pressure to get the fishes attention. The buck King rolled to the surface and sped back in my direction. He played right into my hands which allowed me to close ground, get below him and tire this semi bright fish while leading him into the shallows to where I could tail him.

To my surprise a good friend who was down stream of me, that I was unaware of, had strolled up to where I was putting the finishing touches on this catch with a net. He captured it which was great because I don't want big fish banging around on the rocks while trying to release him. Instead we were able to lead the fish into deeper water to keep him afloat and unhook him. Bill really liked the fly. Bill is also an accomplished wildlife artist, and he knew we were at the Hall of Fame induction event, and he asked about an artist friend the famous accomplished Bill Elliot who also was inducted.

I started to laugh out loud and my friend Bill tilted his head in question on what was so amusing. I explained that Elliot, upon seeing my wife Lindsay standing in the Atrium of the induction building came running over yelling out "Lindsay Lindsay" it's Bill Elliot I've been dying to meet you. You have to understand my lovely wife has become nationally known through social media the many Fly Fishing, Sports Person of the Year awards and National attention with CFR, PHW and TU as a highly accomplished fly angler. Of course as I explained to my friend Bill I was fairly dumbfounded that Hall of Fame folks were seeking out Lindsay. To which Bill stepped back and delivered one of the best lines of the day and maybe for all time as far as I'm concerned. He said "Dave, you have to face it, Lindsay is Famous".

We both laughed, let the fish go, and shook hands me thanking Bill for the help. As common "Swing" etiquette I now climbed up the bank and retreated up river to allow Lind's to have the lead to the tail of the run in hopes of her getting the next pull. But as I walked back down, I knew what had just happened. I had received the KARMA that John bestowed upon me. I could have spent the rest of the afternoon on the bank looking at a couple of bald eagles that were playing in the skies over the river and watch my wife fish. Lindsay's asked what the fish took, and I yelled out Tissa. Anybody within ear shot wouldn't have the slightest idea what the TISSA Fly looked like and not that I was keeping it a secret. Lindsay fished her swing down through the run and I dropped in again.

As I neared the tail out, I saw some commotion that could only mean a small pod of fish had just jumped up through the frothy fast water below into the sanctuary of the meadow run with its deeper slower current. By now I was fishing a flesh fly in hopes that maybe a dime bright steelhead was shadowing these kings looking for some eggs or flesh from some of the Salmon carcasses that littered the stream bed.

Nearly in the same spot as fish number one, the second fish crushed the fly at the apex of the swing. As this big hen clobbered the fly she must have been accompanied by several Suters and her angry reaction to the sting of iron in her jaw blew up the water all around her as fish jolted out of her way. Angry hens both Salmon and Steelhead seem to have much more attitude then the boys. She was upset, and showed that in a blistering run out of the tail and downstream towards the fast water. I had to try and not let her get in there or she would take me back to the estuary. And that wouldn't be a fun run over a quarter mile away.

I scrambled to the bank , and got adjacent to her and once again coxed her up stream with downstream side pressure so she'd want to go up stream. But she was determined not to give in to my unfriendly welcome of her entering this river. Several moments of give and take passed, which made time for Lindsay to come down to me with her tailing glove on. This fish was a beast, and my petite wife had trouble grasping her tail handle with her little hands and subduing the hen in the shallow water gravel. She was all of 30 pounds and over a yard long. I was exhausted as this river is not an easy one to wade let alone try and run around in. We recorded the event for prosperity and sent her on her way to hopefully hook back up with her buck harem she had collected before our "encounter".

Thanks to Gierach's good Vibes

I looked at my lovely wife, and simply stated Karma. This is the Karma that John Gierach had bestowed upon me. And for a couple of fish that he fancied as well.

16

Labrador

LOOKING UP AT the jumble of clouds that resembled a pile of boxes and junk in an unkempt attic, they started to break up and the sun began to peak through. We had a slow start to our day, but had just put three nice Brook trout in the net in under 10 minutes. It was lunch time, and as we unwrapped the gourmet sandwiches that Roseanne had made us that morning, Alvin our guide saw a fish slash the surface 30 feet away. I said to Lindsay since she was in the front of the boat, "Hey take a shot at that fish." Fish had disappeared, but Lind's had him measured up and his position locked into her GPS brain. The Green Drake size 10 dry was false casted a couple times and she landed the fly in the target zone. The big drake idled on the slightly riffled surface for less than five seconds and ever so slightly was sipped under. Lind's ripped her rod into a tight arc, and a four pound brute crashed the surface head shaking and rolling away from the boat in an effort to free himself. She finally led the highly colored up male into the mesh of the net and we joked about this little lunch time bonus fish.

Just after the release Alvin and I saw a second fish slash the surface, some 70 feet away. We had a stiff tail wind so the forward cast was easy, but for this distance I'd have to haul pretty hard on my back cast. Laid down my lunch, took the same rod from Lindsay, same fly,

cranked up a cast had the landing zone locked in, and by gosh got the fly out to where we thought he was hanging.

But instead of a polite little sip of the fly ...a five pound trout came completely out of the water a foot from the fly, gills flared, his entire body parallel to the surface as he steamrolled the fly like a mountain lion pouncing on a deer. The little six weight was bent to the handle and the fish ran off like a steelhead. All week we had been catching these big trout from 3 to nearly 8 pounds and because we had never caught Brook Trout remotely this big before, the pleasure was heightened due to how strong they were.

Lindsay, stands in Steelhead rivers in barely above freezing water all winter long. Climbs in mountains fishing tiny streams, having to make pin point casts. Stands on the bow of a boat in LI Sound firing casts into a head wind to marauding Stripers and False Albi's.... but when it's time to photo a fish, she turns from hearty fly angler in all her foul weather gear, back into the stunningly pretty lady I married. Meaning while the fish is in the net in the water, she fixes her hair, and readies herself for a "Get Your Attention" (complete with holding the fish with her painted nails) photo. Honestly Alvin and I had done this "OK let me get set" photo shoot process so many times that week, we busted her chops to put her long blonde hair in a braid, to end the "Fixing". The fish was never in harm's way gently resting in the net in the water, but we had to wait until our star was ready for her cameo shot with Mr or Mrs. Brook Trout.

Now again, this is my life. Lindsay once caught a 10 pound Lake Ontario brown trout swinging a streamer in the current of a river, while fixing her hair and the rod between her knees because she saw me filming her. She said "I have to loosen my hat, with the braids now, my hat is too tight". She had just casted her fly 30 feet, put the rod in her arm pit, and while adjusting her hat, hooked and landed a six pound trout.

For the next three hours, Lindsay and I took turns. One person on the camera the other on the rod, and we caught fish after fish as they showed themselves on the surface. I caught one last fish on a Salmon bomber fly, and we reeled in as the bright yellow De-Havilland Beaver broke over the tree line on the far end of the lake to come in and retrieve us.

Living in the State of New York, there are very few places you can find and fish to Brook trout that are bigger than a size that would fit in your shirt pocket. The Adirondacks still has some ponds, lakes and rivers where you can expect to catch a brook trout measured in pounds instead of ounces. Many of those places are so secretive that most will never fish them. I know friends who have such places stashed away, and won't share them with us...and hardly even family members.

Lindsay and I love brook trout. They are a heritage fish in our region of the US, but have long since been diminished through the industrial revolution, and modernization. Every year we make a trip to the North Central PA to fish the beautiful mountain streams, many the size one could jump over to catch wild Brookies that if you get an 8 incher, you have a trophy. Anything over that, you are considering a wall mount. Not only are they extremely beautiful, they are willing and aggressive and well....not hard to catch.

Since I was a little kid I read the stories of adventurers like Lee Wulff who would fly off to the great north and find these wild rivers and lakes or ponds teaming with Brook trout that averaged over four pounds with fish pushing the 10 pound range. Trout that had never seen a human before let alone a hand tied fly. The stories from Field and Stream and Sports Afield of these great adventures to and towards the Arctic Circle filled my head with dreams of getting there one day.

Several years ago, Lind's and I sat down and decided to be determined to get to the places on our bucket list. That we'd make the sacrifices (like lavish dinners, and spending money foolishly on things we didn't need like new (Cloths, furniture, or appliances) and save our pennies to take these wished for trips. We've been fortunate to cross a few off the list. The one that had been on there for a while was World Class Brook Trout and we knew that Labrador was the Mecca of full filling that bucket.

We attend the North East Fly fishing show every year in New Jersey. This is the ultimate candy/toy store for fly fishing junkies that includes 100's of outfitters to every type of fly fishing destination you can think of. While Lindsay was busy helping with some Women's events at the show, I was on point to find us that Labrador trip. Number one goal was to find an outfitter who could provide the opportunity to get after the biggest Brookies on the planet, but we were also interested in possibly flying out to an Atlantic Salmon river. I interviewed five outfitters and finally found Jim Burton of Igloo Lake Lodge. Jim has had this lodge in his family for 44 years. He has flown for over 40 years and owns a 1951 in mint condition De-Havilland Beaver where he can get us to both Brook Trout lakes as well as Salmon Rivers.

I brought Lindsay back to Jim's booth and we discussed our goals for the trip, and since Jim was about to do a mini seminar on his operation, we followed him to his talk, and met some others who had been to Igloo Lake with Jim. We asked more detailed and pointed questions and interviewed some references live and in person. We dropped the deposit on Jim that day, and once home from the show started to plan for this trip that was only six months away.

My only reservations on airline travel is I want to carry my Rods and Reels and flies onboard the plane with me. I know I can do that in the domestic US, but we'd be starting this trip in Canada flying out of Toronto since we live only a couple hours from there. Checking the CA-TSA they had the very same descriptions on what one could carry on the plane when it came to fishing gear as the US-TSA. Neither mention Fishing reels,

So we get to Toronto's Pearson International and it's purely out of control or so it appeared. You had to figure out which section our airlines had was for Canadian domestic travel, not flights leaving Canada for other countries. Then the lines were long even though we got there 2 and a half hours before our flight. BUT Air Canada had a process. If you were getting near your departure and you hadn't checked your luggage, they'd pull you out of line and move you to the front. So we made it through with about an hour to spare before takeoff.

Still had to go through TSA. They did riffle through my carry on but no issues and we were home free. We travel cross country to destinations like Alaska routinely and this trip though not as many miles, was going to take all day because of a four hour layover in St John's Newfoundland. Arriving into St. John's was much like flying into the coast of the United Kingdom, with its giant "Cliffs Of Dover" shore line.

Lind's and I are usually entertained in Airports. Always people watching, browsing the shops, a midday lunch and cocktail, an opportunity to catch up on work and emails, or read a good book. St John's airport in staying behind the TSA checkpoint afforded us maybe 50 yards of isle way, with two or three food choices, and a magazine stand. FOUR HOURS. After hour one and having exhausted the four shops we could visit, reading, working and emails, we decided to get our steps in. Creating a walking track route around the three or four gates, and shops.

Eventually boarded a twin engine prop plan, to fly into Deer lake and drop off some folks, and pick up some others making the connection to Goose Bay. The Goose Bay connection out of Toronto, was an hour late and now we had the Deer lake Airport that might be 30 steps of area to hang out in as the pilot decided to wait for the late arrivals.

Finally on the ground in Goose Bay 12 and a half hours after arriving at the Toronto Airport, we were met by Lodge Owner Jim Burton who ferried us to our hotel. Hotel North from the outside looks like a warehouse storage facility (which I guess you can say is an offhand definition of a hotel, a place to store people). However once inside, it was very clean. The rooms were elegant, and the bar restaurant was fun because you met many people traveling through Goose Bay, either working out in the wild or on a fishing trip like us. Goose Bay has a large population of Native Canadians, as well as an Air Force base that was a safety Zone during 9/11 for US Military aircraft.

Take off on Sat morning at Noon was delayed due to weather till 2:30 PM, and then the 40 minute flight had us in the Lodge before dinner. Roseann the camp Chef , and caretaker and who was up at 5 AM to start the coffee, and rebuild the fire in the big wood stove served us a nice early dinner after we squared our gear away, knowing we'd all be chomping at the bit to get in some evening fishing.

There is a pretty little stream running behind the lodge. It's loaded with Brook Trout. All sizes from young of the year to eight pound adults. Lind's and I caught fish at will on dries and streamers. Nothing too big, but all bigger then we have in the States. We met our guide Alvin a resident of Newfoundland and longtime Salmon guide now in his third year with Jim's operation. Alvin was a fairly quiet shy character to begin with, most likely due to his having to weigh Lindsay and my fly fishing capabilities. Once he saw Lindsay uncork her first cast, I could see the calmness wash over him, probably thinking this might be a pretty easy week.

After the first day of catching nice pike on the fly, and some decent Brook trout in the stream, we awoke on day two, to some nasty weather. Cold, 20 MPH winds, gusts to 30, and a rather bleak outlook for the day. The lake was fishable, but there was also an opportunity to fly over to Burton Pond. The others in camp opted to stay put and fish the stream behind the lodge. Lind's and I live for riding around in classic legendary Bush planes in search of fish in remote places.

Jim is nothing short of an excellent pilot. In a 30 MPH breeze he has to land the Beaver, idle up towards the moored fishing boat, cut the engine at the perfect moment so we gently glide up to the boat, without sliding past, to where we have to jump out onto the pontoons and onto the deck of the 16 foot Lund awaiting us. Nicely done, and we are aboard, rigged and ready to fish.

I guess the others back at camp passed on this fly out due to the heavy winds, but these ponds (the size of lakes) have several islands strewn about and you can get leeward of the wind and find calm waters and raising fish. We started by trolling toward some of those Islands and sure enough picked up a few nice four or five pound trout on our flies. Once in position and a bay full of boulders the size of Volkswagen's, we cast and stripped our Muddler Minnows over those structures and were jumped by several big Brook trout looking to chase and kill a moving fly.

As often happens to me fishing with Lindsay, she was lighting up fish after fish, while I was doing more watching and picture taking and NOT lighting up fish. And then the bugs started to come off, Brown Drakes, Green Drakes, and the fish were making those splashy rises one knows as trout eating emergers. I had one little magnetic box in my bag with some size 10 emerger wet flies. These flies are meant for your run of the mill stream trout of maybe 14 to 16 inches. Not 4 to 6 pounds. But as I flicked a wet fly into the fray, it was met with approval, and deep bends in my rod, with the old Hardy singing that sweet music. For once I had the fly and was closing the distance on my beautiful fish catching wife.

The wind was stiff, a few showers passed through, wind chill most likely in the high 40's low 50's, and still the fish were coming up top. Alvin looked at his watch, and said we had to get back closer to the mooring site as the plane would be back to get us soon. We motored over to this nice little cove again leeward of the breeze. It was time for a pee break. The hard thing about a pee break in this place is every island has scrub pines right to the water's edge. It's a massive tangle of ferns, tundra and rock. You have to bush whack your way onto enough turf to take a pee. Especially hard if you are a lady, but among all the marvelous traits, skills Lindsay has, she can pee outside in the wild anywhere ...any time. However, this place was a bit of a challenge.

I was back to the boat first, saw a fish slash, fired a cast, hard take, and another 6 pounder in the net. Out of the corner of my eye, another surface slash, quick cast rifled in, and it's twin was hooked and landed. Now Lind's is back from the ultimate out door ladies room, and she lights up the last fish of the day, just as we heard the low growl of the 51 Beaver break over the tree line on the far shore of the Pond.

All fish are beautiful, but these are "Run Way Models"

Chilly, a bit damp, but having a pond the size of a lake all to ourselves and dozens of world class Brook Trout, we clambered aboard the plane, tired with wide gap smiles on our faces told Jim we had done well. As Jim idled up to the Lodge dock, some other members of the Lodge party were there to greet us. While I'm sure they missed us, they were looking for intel. I was the first to offer, that Burton Pond was a bust and not a destination they'd want to waste their time on, but nobody was buying it, because we couldn't hide the shit eating grins on our faces.

Exquisite Beauty. (There's those RED nails again)

Roseann had held dinner for us, and it wasn't just any dinner. She had cooked a full blown turkey thanksgiving meal, with all the trimmings. All I could think of on the flight back to the lodge after 8 hours in the wind, rain, and stormy skies, was a hot cup of her strong camp coffee. Mix in this turkey dinner, and it truly was a days end thanksgiving.

The next day after our Burton Pond experience we awoke to 40 MPH winds, three to four foot seas on Igloo lake. Was looking like a blow off day. Yet in this place you've never truly out of business with a small river 100 steps away and thousands of brook trout and some nice pike along the entire river.

However, Lindsay and I decided on a quiet day. Drank some coffee, Sat by the fire, read a little, napped, snacked and after dinner hit the river behind the lodge to at least get a bend in a rod. Nobody flew out that day or hit Igloo Lake in the boats as it was too rough. But it calmed down in the evening and everybody fished in one format or the other. I had such great success on a particular streamer in the river. These wild 12 to 20 inch Brookies just hammered a swung fly. And even without a hatch, if you drifted a surface fly through a likely spot you'd certainly get a reaction strike.

At one point I may have caught nearly a dozen fish in as many casts on this streamer, somehow feeling a bit guilty of over staying my welcome I reeled in and sat on the bank to drink in the beauty of this wild place.

Last day of the trip we could have taken a third trip to Burton Lake where we knew we'd probably put a couple dozen trophy Brook Trout in the net. Instead we chose to try and catch a true Monster on Igloo Lake which had recently given up a pair of 10 pounders . We caught a few Pike, and Lindsay did turn and hook a sizable trout that shook free. But the day was more so a wrap up with Guide Alvin trading stories and lots of laughs about our week and other past fishing and traveling experiences.

Reflecting on this trip there was only one downside, if you are un-prepared. The Black Flies! They are the real deal. They are out if its sunny, cloudy, raining, cold, or warm. We had some hand wipes called BugX30. I understand the US Fish and Wildlife service use these when in the wild doing field work. They come in a foil pack so you can wipe them on, and reuse them throughout the day. They were very good. I even fixed one to the brim of my cap and it kept the nasty relentless bugs at bay. But bug suits, or head nets with summer buffs, hooded fishing shirts are a must. As well as fishing gloves. If Labrador is on your bucket list be prepared for the flies.

Early next morning we boarded the Otter and flew back to Goose

Bay in route to Toronto. Another check in the box on the bucket list. Wilds of Labrador, location of the biggest on average Brook Trout in the world, Caught dozens of trophy fish, wonderful guides, hosts and accommodations, making of new friends....CHECK!

Sunset over Igloo Lake